AMERICAN WAR LIBRARY

★ ★ ★ ★

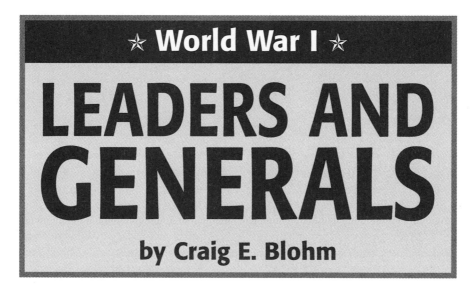

★ World War I ★

LEADERS AND GENERALS

by Craig E. Blohm

Lucent Books, P.O. Box 289011, San Diego, CA 92198-9011

Titles in The American War Library series include:

World War II
Hitler and the Nazis
Kamikazes
Leaders and Generals
Life as a POW
Life of an American Soldier in
  Europe
Strategic Battles in Europe
Strategic Battles in the Pacific
The War at Home
Weapons of War

The Civil War
Leaders of the North and South
Life Among the Soldiers and
  Cavalry
Lincoln and the Abolition of
  Slavery
Strategic Battles
Weapons of War

For Desiree

Library of Congress Cataloging-in-Publication Data

Blohm, Craig E., 1948–
    Leaders and generals / by Craig E. Blohm.
        p. cm. — (American war library. World War I)
Includes bibliographical references and index.
Summary: Discusses John J. Pershing, general of the armies; Erich Ludendorff, a troubled general; Philippe Pétain, hero of Verdun; William "Billy"
Mitchell, prophet of airpower; Douglas Haig, the gentleman soldier; Ferdinand Foch, the will to win; and Woodrow Wilson, crusader for peace.
    ISBN 1-56006-839-6 (alk paper)
    1. World War, 1914–1918—Biography—Juvenile literature. 2. Generals—
Biography—Juvenile literature. 3. Heads of state—Biography—Juvenile
literature. [1. World War, 1914–1918. 2. Generals. 3. Heads of state.]I. Title. II. Series.
    D507 .B56 2002
    940.3'092'2—dc21

                                                                2001000854

Copyright 2002 by Lucent Books, Inc.
P.O. Box 289011, San Diego, California 92198-9011

Printed in the U.S.A.

★ Contents ★

A Nation Forged by War

The United States, like many nations, was forged and defined by war. Despite Benjamin Franklin's opinion that "There never was a good war or a bad peace," the United States owes its very existence to the War of Independence, one to which Franklin wholeheartedly subscribed. The country forged by war in 1776 was tempered and made stronger by the Civil War in the 1860s.

The Texas Revolution, the Mexican-American War, and the Spanish-American War expanded the country's borders and gave it overseas possessions. These wars made the United States a world power, but this status came with a price, as the nation became a key but reluctant player in both World War I and World War II.

Each successive war further defined the country's role on the world stage. Following World War II, U.S. foreign policy redefined itself to focus on the role of defender, not only of the freedom of its own citizens, but also of the freedom of people everywhere. During the cold war that followed World War II until the collapse of the Soviet Union, defending the world meant fighting communism. This goal, manifested in the Korean and Vietnam conflicts, proved elusive, and soured the American public on its achievability. As the United States emerged as the world's sole superpower, American foreign policy has been guided less by national interest and more on protecting international human rights. But as involvement in Somalia and Kosovo prove, this goal has been equally elusive.

As a result, the country's view of itself changed. Bolstered by victories in World Wars I and II, Americans first relished the role of protector. But, as war followed war in a seemingly endless procession, Americans began to doubt their leaders, their motives, and themselves. The Vietnam War especially caused people to question the validity of sending its young people to die in places where they were not particularly wanted and for people who did not seem especially grateful.

While the most obvious changes brought about by America's wars have been geopolitical in nature, many other aspects of society have been touched. War often does not bring about change directly, but acts instead like the catalyst in a chemical reaction, accelerating changes already in progress.

Some of these changes have been societal. The role of women in the United States had been slowly changing, but World War II put thousands into the workforce and into uniform. They might have gone back to being housewives after the war, but equality, once experienced, would not be forgotten.

Likewise, wars have accelerated technological change. The necessity for faster airplanes and a more destructive bomb led to the development of jet planes and nuclear energy. Artificial fibers developed for parachutes in the 1940s were used in the clothing of the 1950s.

Lucent Books' American War Library covers key wars in the development of the nation. Each war is covered in several volumes, to allow for more detail, context, and to provide volumes on often neglected subjects, such as the kamikazes of World War II, or weapons used in the Civil War. As with all Lucent Books, notes, annotated bibliographies, and appendixes such as glossaries give students a launching point for further research. In addition, sidebars and archival photographs enhance the text. Together, each volume in The American War Library will aid students in understanding how America's wars have shaped and changed its politics, economics, and society.

"Lions Led by Donkeys"

For a week the relentless pounding of Allied artillery hammered at the German defenses, some of the strongest on the Western Front. Now, on July 1, 1916, British and French soldiers climbed out of their protective trenches and walked into the withering machine gunfire of the German army. The Battle of the Somme had begun.

The Somme was one of the major battles in the global conflict known as the Great War or, as we now call it, World War I. In the late nineteenth and early twentieth centuries, many nations formed alliances, or partnerships, for political and economic reasons. Two major alliances emerged: the Central Powers (Germany, Austria-Hungary, and Turkey, among others) and the Allied Powers (which included France, Great Britain, Russia, and the United States). In June 1914, Archduke Franz Ferdinand of Austria-Hungary was assassinated, igniting the war that would last four years and claim nearly 30 million

soldiers dead and wounded. It was the most devastating war the world had yet seen.

The Battle of the Somme raged for nearly five months. In the end casualties on the Allied side reached some 600,000, all for a small gain in territory with no particular strategic significance. On that first bloody day alone the British army suffered more than 57,000 dead and wounded. Such appalling losses were due in large part to the inadequate and sparse training of the British soldier and the incompetent command of his officers. "The British were right to be on the Somme," writes military historian Richard Holmes, "but so many of them would not lie there today had some of their leaders shown a moral courage equal to the physical valor of the men they commanded."[1]

Legend has it that one German officer described the British forces at the Somme as "lions led by donkeys." It is unclear who may have made this statement, which has

British soldiers climb out of a trench during the Battle of the Somme, one of the major battles of World War I.

been variously attributed to General Erich Ludendorff, his Chief of Staff Colonel Max Hoffmann, or possibly even Kaiser Wilhelm. Richard Holmes suggests that it may refer to a German comment about French soldiers during the Franco-Prussian War (1870–71).

But who said it, or whether it was even said at all, is less important than the question it raises: Were the generals of World War I "donkeys" leading their brave but inexperienced "lions" to the slaughter? Were the men who planned the strategy and tactics of the war so heartless and incompetent that they would send thousands of young soldiers to certain death in order to gain a few yards of mud, and possibly gain a few medals for their own glory? The military leaders of World War I were only human, of course, subject to the same forces and frailties that affect us all. The difference lies in the fact that these leaders were given the power of life and death in a war of unprecedented enormity. Each would handle that power in his own way.

Military discipline requires that a certain distance be kept between soldiers and their commanders. In World War I that distance could seem like an unfathomable abyss. We often find the words "cold," "arrogant," and "aloof" used to describe World War I generals. While the ordinary soldier fought not only the enemy but disease, rats, and lice in the filthy trenches of the Western Front, the lives of their commanders-in-chief often resembled that of high society. Their headquarters were normally established in rambling châteaux far behind the battle lines. They dined on fine food and wine while their men's meals were often barely edible. Chauffeurs drove

them to and from the front, and they often had time to indulge in golf or other recreations.

Yet, like their men, the commanders of World War I were thrust into a kind of warfare that no one in the world had experienced before. These generals were all products of the nineteenth-century military establishment, when war meant row upon row of infantry marching straight and proud into battle, and when horses were essential for transporting supplies

World War I troops experienced a new kind of warfare with the development of weapons such as the machine gun and poisonous gas.

and ammunition to the front. But with this new war came new technologies of destruction: machine guns that could mow down a line of soldiers in seconds, airplanes that dueled in graceful but deadly dogfights high above the front, and poison gas that would kill a man almost before he knew what was happening. Instead of troops advancing in ranks through open fields, soldiers now hid in trenches, only rarely venturing "over the top" to face almost certain death in the barren waste between the front lines known as "no man's land." It would take much time and cost countless lives before the generals of World War I learned to cope with these new ways of waging war.

To be sure, commanders were often in the thick of battle; nearly sixty general officers died in the war. More often, however, a general who didn't produce satisfactory results was relieved of his command, replaced with another who would also stand or fall on his merits. It was a dilemma that many commanders faced: Should they send in more troops to gain an objective, knowing that failure meant young lives wasted and a career most likely in ruins? Sometimes the gamble paid off. At other times it meant nothing but massive casualties, like those suffered at the Battle of the Somme.

Of the seven men profiled here, six spent their lives waging war; the seventh was a president intent on bringing peace to a world shattered by war. Each had the power to send young men into battle for political ideals. The "lions" proved their courage at places that, to us, bear strange names: Verdun and Château-Thierry, the Marne and Ypres. The "donkeys" led their men, sometimes into brilliant triumph, more often into utter disaster. But whether victorious or defeated, the leaders and generals of World War I charted the course of a war that changed the world forever.

Chapter 1

John J. Pershing: General of the Armies

aris had never seen such a crowd, at least not in recent memory. It was the afternoon of June 13, 1917. Thousands of people swarmed through the streets, forcing the official motorcade to slow to a crawl. Old men, veterans of wars fought long ago, and young men maimed in the present one waved American flags and handkerchiefs in salute. Women wept and tossed flowers. Children shinnied up lampposts and trees, frantically waving and shouting to the cars below. Cries of *"Vive l'Amérique!"* filled the air: "Long live America!" As the lead car of the motorcade crept along, an American general peered out, stunned at the spectacle that swirled around him. He responded to the cries and shouts of the multitude with a small wave and a forced smile. General John Joseph "Black Jack" Pershing, commander of the American Expeditionary Forces (AEF), had come to save France, to finally win the "war to end wars." As his car slowly moved through the crowd, General Pershing began to truly feel the weight of the great responsibility that had been thrust upon him.

Accepting responsibility was second nature for John Joseph Pershing. He was a tireless worker who pushed his subordinates to work hard as well. Too hard, some would complain. At Pershing's headquarters in France, even Sundays meant work as usual. Many soldiers regarded him as cold-hearted and inaccessible, a forbidding person who required respect, but inspired fear. A colleague once described Pershing with the words "cold, intellectual, unhuman."[2] Yet he had another side, one that seldom appeared when he was on duty. Pershing could be warm and personable, a modest and sensitive man when among friends. For some reason, he was either unwilling or unable to reveal this aspect of his personality to his troops.

In a war fought on foreign soil John J. Pershing set out to create a separate American army. It was a daunting task for he had

11

to build, organize, and train an army practically from the ground up. Resisting the efforts of Allied commanders to use American troops as mere replacements in their lines, Pershing turned his inexperienced recruits into efficient fighting soldiers that ultimately helped secure the Allied victory.

For John J. Pershing it was important "to have something worthwhile to do, and to do it with all there is in me—no matter what the circumstances."[3] The circumstances that would shape the life and career of John Joseph Pershing began in a turbulent period of American history.

Missouri Farm Boy

Missouri in 1860 was a state situated on the edge of a divided America, a nation that would soon be embroiled in its own terrible war. Torn between slavery and the Union, Missourians feared the coming Civil War perhaps more than people in other states did. It was into this climate that John Joseph Pershing was born near the small town of Laclede on September 13, 1860. His father, John Fletcher Pershing, worked for the Hannibal and St. Joseph Railroad and was firmly against slavery. Although his mother, Anne, came from a Confederate family, she shared her husband's loyalty to the Union.

By the time the Civil War had come and gone, young John was leading the life of a typical Missouri farm boy. There were chores, of course, but schooling was also important. John studied the basics of reading, writing, and arithmetic, first with his mother as his teacher and later at a one-room public school.

General John Joseph "Black Jack" Pershing was considered a forbidding person who inspired fear among his men.

Pershing entered the United States Military Academy at West Point in 1882. Over a hundred years later, the academy continues to train cadets for military service.

For a while the Pershing family flourished. But in 1873 a severe depression hit, wiping out much of the family's wealth and forcing John's father to go on the road as a traveling salesman. This left John, as the eldest child, to manage the family farm full-time. "These years," he later recalled, "were really worth while for me, as difficult as they were. I learned more of the practical side of life than during any similar period."[4] It was his first taste of real responsibility and so, at age thirteen, he began to understand what it was to do his duty.

West Point

Eventually the Pershing land had to be sold, and John began looking for a job. In 1878 he passed a county examination and re-

ceived a teaching certificate. He taught at a school for black children in Laclede, and later at a white school in Prairie Mound some ten miles away. Able to save some money each month from his pay, John began planning his future. He enrolled in the normal school at Kirksville, Missouri, in order to improve his teaching skills. This way he figured he could make enough money to someday attend law school. One day John read an announcement about an upcoming examination to nominate a candidate for the Military

Academy at West Point. While John had had no prior thoughts of pursuing a military career, he felt that an academy education would be good preparation for law school. He passed the exam, and on July 1, 1882, John Pershing entered the United States Military Academy at West Point.

At West Point, John studied trigonometry, geography, philosophy, and French as well as such military disciplines as horsemanship, musketry, tactics, and, of course, marching. As he trained to be a soldier, John still thought about entering the legal profession. But at some point the academy motto, "Duty, Honor, Country," must have penetrated his soul. Academically, Pershing was never outstanding, ranking only midway in his graduating class. But he was beginning to display the qualities of a leader: courage, self-control, and devotion to duty. His strict style of leadership earned him few close friends. Fellow cadet Robert W. Bullard later recalled that Pershing "inspired confidence but not affection. . . . His exercise of authority was . . . impersonal, dispassionate, hard and firm."[5]

By the time he graduated on June 12, 1886, John Pershing was First Captain of the Corps of Cadets. It was the highest cadet office and a position of honor. Of the seventy-seven cadets graduating that day, fifty-nine would still be alive when the United States entered World War I. But only one of them, the former farm boy and teacher from Laclede, Missouri, would be given the daunting task of leading the American army to victory.

Early Military Exploits

The road that ultimately led Pershing to Paris that spring in 1917 had taken him through numerous battles both near and far. After the Civil War the U.S. Army had turned its attention to the problem of protecting settlers moving west from attacks by hostile Native Americans. In 1886 Lieutenant Pershing was given command of the Sixth Cavalry Regiment and spent the next five years chasing Apache and Sioux tribes across what would become New Mexico, Arizona, and South Dakota. After a stint teaching military science at the University of Nebraska, Pershing took command of the Tenth Cavalry, a regiment made up of black soldiers. This command would eventually earn Pershing the nickname "Black Jack," a name that would follow him for the rest of his life.

In 1897 Pershing found himself back at West Point, this time as an assistant instructor in tactics. The cadets found him cold and arrogant, an unforgiving taskmaster. Perhaps he believed the cadets would adopt his own high standards of conduct. But Pershing's strict rules and excessive handing out of demerits for minor infractions only earned him their animosity. Upon entering the crowded dining hall one day, Pershing was greeted with utter stillness. Called "the silence," it was the cadets' most extreme display of disapproval for an officer. Pershing would spend less than a year teaching at West Point before requesting a transfer. Rumors of war in Cuba were brewing, and he was eager to see action once more.

The Spanish-American War in 1898 gave John Pershing his first experience in combat on foreign soil. Commanding the Tenth Cavalry, Pershing and his troops stormed San Juan Hill beside Teddy Roosevelt's Rough Riders. Pershing performed admirably in battle, one commander calling him "cool as a bowl of cracked ice."[6] With the United States victorious in the Spanish-American War, control of the Philippine Islands was transferred from Spain to America. In 1899 Pershing was sent to keep the peace in the Philippines. Half a world away from home, Pershing enthusiastically carried out his duties. "There is a romance about it all," he said, ". . . being ready to serve the country when it calls, the exhilaration of keeping physically fit, the stimulus of competition with one's fellows . . . all add zest to army life."[7] Apart

from several excursions to the United States (during one, he married Helen Frances Warren) and a trip to Japan to observe the Russo-Japanese War, the Philippines would be Pershing's home for the next fifteen years.

Telegram and Tragedy

John J. Pershing's first hint that he might enter World War I came in the form of a telegram in 1917 from his father-in-law, Senator Francis E. Warren. With peace restored and the Philippine insurrection finally quelled, Pershing was once more back in the United States. While stationed in Texas he had spent a year pursuing the notorious guerrilla Pancho Villa through the badlands of northern Mexico. This "punitive expedition" gave Pershing and his troops valuable

In 1886 Pershing was given command of a cavalry regiment like this one.

military experience. He was able to try out new tactics and solve logistical problems in deploying the largest force he had ever commanded. The expedition was also a testing ground for the machinery of modern warfare: trucks, radios, machine guns, and airplanes. In addition, it provided him with a needed distraction from a terrible personal tragedy. On August 27, 1915, a fire had roared through the Pershing family's living quarters in San Francisco, killing Pershing's wife and three daughters. Only their six-year-old son Warren escaped unharmed. Pershing's grief was intense, and he became more withdrawn and stricter in disciplining his troops. To ease the pain of loneliness, he turned to the familiarity of duty.

Pershing received Senator Warren's telegram on May 3, 1917, at his headquarters in San Antonio, Texas. It was short and to the point: "Wire me today whether and how much you speak, read and write French."[8] It had not been Pershing's best subject at West Point, but he wired back that he could "easily reacquire satisfactory working knowledge."[9]

The United States had declared war on Germany on April 6, 1917, and on May 27 Pershing received written orders from Secretary of War Newton D. Baker: "You [will] command all the land forces of the United States operating in Continental Europe and in the United Kingdom of Great Britain and Ireland. . . ."[10] The Allied commanders expected to use American troops as replacements in their own battle lines. But Pershing's orders specified that "the

Pershing acquired invaluable military experience while pursuing guerrilla Pancho Villa (pictured) through Mexico.

forces of the United States are a separate and distinct component of the combined forces, the identity of which must be preserved."[11] The next day, General John J. "Black Jack" Pershing set sail for Europe and World War I.

Americans in Paris

Three years of bloody warfare had exhausted the French army both physically and mentally. Morale was at its lowest ebb since the beginning of hostilities. Two million casualties had been sustained in a stalemate fought in the mud-clogged, blood-soaked trenches of the Western Front. And now, many French units had simply given up, refusing to continue fighting in the useless slaughter that the war had become.

One of Pershing's first duties was to confer with the leaders of the Allied forces.

On June 16 Pershing met with General Henri Philippe Pétain, the French commander in Chief. The two men had similar personalities and hit it off right away. After the war, during a difficult time for Pétain, Pershing would remark, "This general is the greatest of the war."[12] But now, as the two leaders dined together, the French general expressed a sentiment that was on many minds: "I hope," Pétain said, "it is not too late."[13]

"Lafayette, We Are Here!"

Throughout history, America's wars have produced their share of heroes and cowards, brilliant victories and stunning defeats. Wars also produce some of the most memorable phrases ever uttered. In its early days, the navy seemed to inspire many of its commanders to memorable expression. When his battle with a British frigate in 1779 seemed all but lost, John Paul Jones defiantly proclaimed, "I have not yet begun to fight!" In the War of 1812, American sailors were inspired by the dying words of Captain James Lawrence: "Don't give up the ship!"

The army, too, has produced its share of unforgettable utterances. During World War II, when General Douglas MacArthur was forced to leave the embattled Philippines, he promised, "I shall return." And he did, nearly two and a half years later. The award for the shortest memorable military quote goes to General Anthony McAuliffe who, upon being asked if he wished to surrender during the Battle of the Bulge in World War II, offered this succinct reply: "Nuts!"

The most memorable saying to come out of World War I was attributed to General John Joseph Pershing. The only problem is, he never said it! On July 4, 1917, French leaders staged a celebration to honor the arrival of Pershing and his troops in France. Later that day, Pershing attended a ceremony at Picpus Cemetery, the final resting place of the Marquis de Lafayette. Lafayette's soldiers had helped the struggling American Continental Army during the Revolutionary War, and it now seemed fitting that American troops had come to the aid of France.

After Pershing made a few short remarks, Colonel Charles E. Stanton gave a speech on behalf of the United States. He closed his address with a pledge that America was about to repay her long-standing debt: "Lafayette, we are here!" It was a perfect phrase that captured the emotion of the moment. It would have been even more perfect had Pershing himself said it. He wrote of the incident in his unpublished memoir, now part of the Pershing Papers in the Library of Congress and quoted here from Frank E. Vandiver's *Illustrious Americans: John J. Pershing*:

> Many have attributed this striking utterance to me, and I have often wished that it could have been mine. But I have no recollection of saying anything so splendid. I am sure those words were spoken by Colonel Stanton and to him must go the credit for coining so happy and felicitous a phrase.

Despite his repeated denials, people would mistakenly ascribe Colonel Stanton's words to General Pershing for the rest of his life.

Later Pershing visited Sir Douglas Haig, the British commander, at his headquarters. As with Pétain, Pershing found he had much in common with Haig. For his part, Haig was impressed with Pershing's "quiet, gentlemanly bearing—so unusual for an American."[14] Together, these three men would in large part be responsible for winning or losing the war for the Allies. None could foresee the difficulties they would have in agreeing how that war should be fought.

The Commanders Disagree

As American troops slowly began arriving in Europe throughout the summer and fall of 1917, the Allied commanders were beginning to wonder if their new partner was up to the task of fighting a world war. By December 1917 there were only about 175,000 U.S. soldiers on French soil, compared with some two and a half million allied troops and more than two million Germans. What's more, the Americans needed additional training before they would be ready for combat. But because of events in Russia, that combat might not wait for American troops to be prepared. Since 1914 Germany had been forced to fight on two fronts: the Western Front against France, Belgium, and Great Britain, and the Eastern Front against Russia. But in November 1917, Russia, in the throes of a political revolution, stopped fighting and signed a peace treaty with Germany. Suddenly thousands of Germany's best soldiers in the east were free to join

the fighting on the Western Front. Such an influx of experienced combat troops could finally turn the tide in favor of Germany. The question was, could they do it before Pershing's army was ready to fight?

To Generals Pétain and Haig, the answer was obvious: American troops should be "amalgamated," or blended in with the Allied forces to strengthen the lines where needed. This plan seemed reasonable on the surface, yet Pershing had many reasons for opposing it. First, American soldiers might question or even resent orders given them by French or British officers. If a battle should end in defeat, the American troops might be blamed for the failure. Also, Pershing worried that support from the American people back home might diminish without a truly American army to rally behind. While Pershing had the authority to amalgamate his troops should a "critical situation" arise, he felt that situation had not yet been reached. The next spring, however, the German army would do its best to bring the war to a critical—and victorious—point.

Spring Offensive

On March 21, 1918, German artillery began a five-hour barrage against the British sector of the Allied front. Then came the infantry, storm troopers who outnumbered and outfought the weary British defenders. The thrust pushed the Western Front, which had virtually remained static throughout the war, some forty miles into Allied territory. The Allied commanders

German soldiers push the Western Front forty miles into Allied territory, convincing Pershing to allow American troops to join the fight.

were shaken; certain defeat seemed to be approaching with the German soldiers. Would Pershing now allow the Americans to join the fight? Despite his determination to build an American army, Pershing could be flexible when necessary. He had already allowed some American regiments to temporarily join Pétain's forces, with the understanding that they would be returned to American control when needed.

On March 28 Secretary of War Newton Baker approved an Allied plan for using American soldiers against the German offensive. Baker and Pershing met and agreed that unless American troops fortified the weakening Allies, the war could be lost. Later that day Pershing visited the French army headquarters. "I have come to tell you," he began, "that the American

people would consider it a great honor for our troops to be engaged in the present battle. I ask you for this in their name and my own. At this moment there are no other questions but of fighting."[15] Pershing's words energized the French military leaders. And they had come none too soon, for less than two weeks later Germany's second assault of the spring offensive began.

An American Army

On August 10, 1918, Pershing achieved his long-awaited dream of a fully independent American army. On that day he took official command of the American First Army with a total strength of over 1,100,000 men. Their initial objective was to attack the salient at a small village named St. Mihiel. A salient was a bulge in the battle line caused by advancing enemy troops.

Pershing was responsible for preparing the largest American military operation in history. He drafted battle plans based on his ideas of dynamic open field fighting rather than the Allies' static trench warfare. He was quick to delegate authority to his subordinates, the mark of an efficient commander. On September 12, 1918, the assault began. After a four-hour artillery barrage, the infantry went "over the top," leaving their trenches to advance on the enemy. From his

vantage point on a nearby hill Pershing watched the battle unfold, filled with pride that his troops, *American* troops, were in the thick of the action. Pershing received reports that "everything was going well, with losses light."[16] Under a punishing assault from American and French troops, St. Mihiel fell the next day, September 13. It was a significant date for Pershing, for on that day he turned fifty-eight years old. What better birthday present could he receive than a victory for the United States Army?

Pershing designed a successful battle plan in which American soldiers advance on enemy troops rather than remain in the trenches.

Well Done . . . And Farewell

The war was over. More than fifty-three thousand American soldiers had given their lives in battle to make the world, in the words of President Woodrow Wilson, "safe for democracy." On November 12, 1918, the day after the armistice was signed, General John J. Pershing paused to reflect on the war and on the fighting men he had commanded. The following is an excerpt from General Order No. 203, written that day by Pershing to the troops of the American Expeditionary Forces. It is taken from *My Experiences in the World War,* Pershing's Pulitzer Prize–winning memoir.

> The enemy has capitulated. It is fitting that I address myself in thanks directly to the officers and soldiers of the American Expeditionary Forces who by their heroic efforts have made possible this glorious result. Our armies, hurriedly raised and hastily trained, met a veteran enemy and by courage, discipline, and skill always defeated him. Without complaint you have endured incessant toil, privation and danger. You have seen many of your comrades make the supreme sacrifice that freedom may live. I thank you for the patience and courage with which you have endured. I congratulate you upon the splendid fruits of victory which your heroism and the blood of our gallant dead are now presenting to our nation. Your deeds will live forever on the most glorious pages of American history.

While most of the soldiers of the AEF would soon be returning home, many would not. Pershing had not forgotten, nor would he ever forget, those who had made the "supreme sacrifice." At an American cemetery in France, he looked out over thousands of crosses dotting the peaceful landscape. As quoted in Donald Smythe's book, *Pershing: General of the Armies,* Pershing solemnly bid farewell to the soldiers who would be left behind:

> And now, Dear Comrades, Farewell. Here, under the clear skies, on the green hillsides and amid the flowering fields of France, in the quiet hush of peace, we leave you forever in God's keeping.

Armistice

The final campaign of the war, the Meuse-Argonne offensive, began on September 26, 1918. Because the battle began soon after St. Mihiel, Pershing had to hurry to get some 600,000 soldiers into position. For forty-seven days American and French troops, aided by artillery, tanks, and airplanes, pounded the German lines. By the time the Germans called for an armistice, some 1,200,000 soldiers of the American Expeditionary Forces had taken part in the battle.

The armistice that took effect on November 11, 1918, ended the fighting career of General John J. Pershing. But even as the terms of the armistice were being hammered out, Pershing again found himself disagreeing with his colleagues. He thought the armistice was a mistake, and wished that the American Expeditionary Forces had been given the opportunity to defeat the German army. The armistice, after all, was merely a truce, not a victory. "The German troops today," Pershing said, "are marching back into Germany announcing that they have never been defeated. . . . What I dread is that Germany doesn't know that she was licked. Had they given us another week, we'd have *taught* them."[17]

Prior to Pershing, George Washington (pictured) was the only other soldier to be commissioned General of the Armies of the United States.

But the war was over and Pershing had to think about his own army, about getting two million men back to America, back to quiet farms and small towns and big cities, back *home*. He traveled across Europe, inspecting his units and pinning medals on proudly worn uniforms. He gave congratulatory speeches to AEF soldiers bound for the troopships that would take them across the Atlantic to be reunited with their families.

Pershing was soon to experience his own reunion. On March 14, 1919, nine-year-old Warren Pershing joined his father in France. Pershing had not seen his son for two years. Their reunion was an emo-

tional one for the general. "Nothing was said particularly," commented Pershing's chauffeur, "but you could see it in the general's eyes—the pride, the love, the feeling that Warren was his and the only thing that he had left."[18]

On September 1, 1919, Pershing and his entourage boarded the ocean liner *Leviathan* for the voyage home. En route a telegram arrived announcing that Congress had voted Pershing the permanent commission of General of the Armies of the United States. It was a rank attained by only one other soldier—George Washington.

After his return home, Pershing spent six weeks in much needed rest and relaxation. Finally he had time to consider what he would do with his remaining years. There was talk of Pershing for president. Many military officers had become president: Washington had, and Andrew Jackson, Zachary Taylor, and Ulysses S. Grant. Although publicly Pershing displayed no interest in holding the nation's highest office, he privately considered the possibility, saying that "no patriotic American could decline to serve in that high position if called to do so by the people."[19] But the call never came, and Pershing went on instead to become the army's chief of staff, a position he held until his retirement from the military at age sixty-four on his birthday, September 13, 1924.

A True Soldier

Pershing spent his retirement years as chairman of the American Battle Monuments Commission, seeing to the proper preservation and commemoration of battlefields and cemeteries where so many young men had been killed and laid to rest. He published a military memoir, a two-volume work entitled *My Experiences in the World War* that won the Pulitzer Prize for history. But Pershing always regretted that the job of the American Expeditionary Forces had been left incomplete and predicted that America would have to do "it all again."[20] These were prophetic words, for soon a corporal who had fought in the German trenches of World War I would begin his rise to political power. That corporal was Adolf Hitler.

When the next war came, General of the Armies John J. Pershing was too old and too frail to fight. Yet many who had served under Pershing became household names during World War II, among them George S. Patton, Douglas MacArthur, and George C. Marshall. As Pershing had celebrated his own victory in 1918, so he lived to witness the Allied victory in 1945. His only regret was being too ill to travel one last time to Europe for the victory celebration. After Pershing's death on July 15, 1948, at the age of eighty-seven, President Harry S. Truman said Pershing "retained the dignity and modest bearing of the true soldier."[21] And so he was. Years before, Pershing had chosen his burial plot at Arlington National Cemetery. "When the last bugle call is sounded," Pershing reportedly said, "I want to stand up with my men."[22] On July 19, 1948, on a hill overlooking the graves of World War I veterans, a lone bugler played taps as John J. "Black Jack" Pershing was lowered to his final resting place. Under a plain standard-issue headstone, the General of the Armies was at last home with his men.

Chapter 2

Erich Ludendorff: A Troubled General

Paul von Hindenburg stood on the platform of the railroad station at Hanover, Germany, the early morning darkness pierced only by the bright lights over the platform. It was August 23, 1914, and the sixty-seven-year-old field marshal had just recently been called out of retirement to command Germany's Eighth Army fighting Russia on the Eastern Front. He wore his old, obsolete, blue uniform, hastily altered by his wife to accommodate an expanding waistline. Now he waited for a train carrying the man who would be his chief of staff, a general he had never met and knew little about.

Around 4 A.M. a special three-car train pulled into the Hanover station and rolled to a stop. Wearing a tailored gray, officer's uniform, General Erich Ludendorff stepped smartly from the train and saluted Hindenburg. The old field marshal returned the salute, then shook Ludendorff's hand. Soon the train was moving again, carrying the two men toward the Eastern Front, and toward a partnership that would not only spearhead Germany's war effort but eventually gain vast political power as well.

It was to be an unequal partnership, however. Although Paul von Hindenburg was the superior officer and nominally the commander in chief, it was Erich Ludendorff who planned the military operations and determined Germany's conduct of the war. Yet he was plagued by an uneven temperament, an inability to compromise, and sudden fits of rage. Ludendorff's fanatical devotion to his convictions would ultimately lead him to embrace some bizarre ideologies later in life.

Erich Ludendorff's brilliance as a tactician inspired military historian Sir Basil Liddell Hart to describe him as "perhaps the greatest of all among the leaders of the War."[23] It was perhaps a strange legacy for a young man whose early years didn't seem to point toward a military career.

Early Life in Prussia

Erich Friedrich Wilhelm Ludendorff was born on April 9, 1865, in Kruszczewina, Prussia, near what today is Poznan in Poland. Unlike most Prussian military officers, who came from aristocratic backgrounds, Erich was raised in a humble, working-class family.

Although General Erich Ludendorff was considered a brilliant tactician, he also possessed an uneven temperament and an inability to compromise.

His father was a landowner and small businessman from a family that had lived in Prussia for more than two hundred years. Prussia, formerly an independent kingdom, became the dominant member of the German Empire in 1871. The third of six children, Erich and his siblings grew up in a modest, white, two-story farmhouse next to an orchard in the quiet German countryside. Erich's early years at the local school showed him to be a good student, especially in mathematics.

Perhaps his surroundings were too quiet, for soon Erich decided that he wanted to pursue a military career. In 1877, at the age of twelve, Erich entered the German Royal Cadet School, scoring high marks on the entrance exam. While he continued to show exceptional achievement in class, Erich was a lonely, withdrawn student. He found it difficult to make friends and preferred the classroom and his studies to sports and other nonacademic activities. This iron self-discipline and obsessive devotion to work above all else would become a significant characteristic of Erich Ludendorff's later military career. After three years at the cadet school, fifteen-year-old Erich entered the Military Academy near Berlin. Again, he immersed himself in study; he wasted no time in idle diversions or the social life that other students enjoyed.

In 1882, at age seventeen, he received his commission as a second lieutenant in the infantry. For the next several years Erich served in various assignments in the peacetime army. The diligent military student became a diligent army officer, a quality that did not go unnoticed by his superiors. Further training prepared Erich for a position as a staff officer, and by 1900 he had been promoted to the rank of major. Erich was pleased with his steady advancement and his promising future. It was a period that he would later describe as "a time I shall never forget."[24] But even greater things were in store for Erich Ludendorff. In 1904 he was summoned to Berlin to join the Supreme General Staff under the great general, Alfred von Schlieffen.

Schlieffen's Disciple

Since 1891 Count Alfred von Schlieffen had been chief of the German General Staff, a group of high-ranking officers charged with planning for and conducting wars. Schlieffen was, in the words of Erich Ludendorff, "one of the greatest soldiers who ever lived."[25] The foundation of Schlieffen's plan was decisive action and swift victory, and Ludendorff wholeheartedly endorsed it. His task as part of the Second Department of the General Staff was to help prepare for mobilizing and deploying troops in the event of hostilities. This he did with his usual determination and self-discipline.

Soon after he officially presented his plan in 1905, Alfred von Schlieffen retired.

He was succeeded as chief of the General Staff by Helmuth von Moltke, an unimaginative general who took the job reluctantly. Under Moltke, Ludendorff's authority grew, and in 1908 he was promoted to chief of the Second Department. Much to his satisfaction, Ludendorff's career was steadily advancing toward more power and influence. Yet even a single-minded career officer could have a gentler side. For Erich Ludendorff, that side was brought out by the woman who would soon become his wife.

Margarethe

Ludendorff met Margarethe Pernet in 1909. His desire to wed her was complicated by the fact that she was already married. But Erich Ludendorff never let obstacles stand in his way, and he persuaded Margarethe to seek a divorce. They were married that same year. Although the couple would have no children, Margarethe had three sons, Franz, Heinz, and Erich, and a daughter, Margot, from her first marriage. Ludendorff was a loving husband, and treated Margarethe's children as his own. They, in turn, accepted their stepfather. "From the beginning," Margarethe wrote, "my children had a warm liking for their new father, and this in the course of the war deepened into love and admiration."[26] Having a new family, however, did not change Ludendorff's compulsive personality. As Margarethe recalled, "Time was not reckoned in our house by hours, but by minutes. He would say for instance, 'Today

I shall be back at four o'clock for some food.' He would come back on the stroke . . . and walk straight into the dining room. If the soup was not already on the table, he would say teasingly, 'Well, there's a nice thing, there's nothing to eat in your well-managed house today.'"[27]

Indeed, Ludendorff would never allow family responsibilities to affect his duty to the German army and its preparations for war.

The Schlieffen Plan

Count Alfred von Schlieffen's plan for war, known simply as the Schlieffen Plan, was designed to fight a two-front war. Germany occupied a vulnerable geographic location between France to the west and Russia to the east. Should armed conflict with these neighboring nations occur at the same time, Germany would have the difficult task of fighting an enemy on each border. Schlieffen's answer to this problem was simple: Germany would mount a swift attack against France, sending a powerful force through Belgium in order to outflank France's fortified border. German troops would then sweep toward Paris and quickly subdue the country. When France was defeated, Germany could turn its full attention to its eastern foe, Russia.

The fact that Belgium was a neutral country and that attacking through it would almost certainly draw Britain into the war did not seem to bother Schlieffen. As quoted in Roger Parkinson's book *Tormented Warrior,* Ludendorff agreed: "We were all convinced of the soundness of this plan. In our unfavorable military-political position in the center of Europe, surrounded by enemies, we had to reckon with foes greatly superior in numbers and prepare ourselves accordingly, if we did not wish to allow ourselves to be crushed."

The Schlieffen Plan might have worked if Schlieffen's successor, Helmuth von Moltke, hadn't changed it, weakening the thrust toward Paris. Schlieffen had estimated that it would take only six weeks to conquer France. But as history shows, the war would drag on for more than four years and end, not with a conquered France, but a defeated Germany.

Count Alfred von Schlieffen designed the Schlieffen Plan, a method for fighting a two-front war.

Planning For War

Ludendorff was well aware that both France and Russia had larger armed forces than Germany. His first task, therefore, was to call for more troops to be recruited. He pressed for additional heavy artillery and increased ammunition production as well as improvements in field communication equipment and aircraft. In his zeal to strengthen the army, Ludendorff would go to any lengths, including political scheming that extended far beyond his military authority. It is no wonder, then, that he made enemies, especially within the German government. When the government approved fewer troops than Ludendorff had requested, he became convinced that the politicians were not willing to fully support the army.

In 1913 Ludendorff was forced out of the General Staff and transferred to an obscure regimental command in Dusseldorf. He spent a year training his troops and participating in war games. In April 1914 he was promoted to major general and took command of the Eighty-fifth Infantry Brigade. Two months later Archduke Franz Ferdinand of Austria was assassinated, the spark that touched off World War I. By July 1914 Ludendorff had returned to the General Staff. He wrote to Margarethe, "I am thirsting for a man's work to do, and it will be given me in full measure. Pray for me, beloved, that my efforts

The assassination of Archduke Franz Ferdinand of Austria was the spark that ignited World War I.

may be crowned with success."[28] Success would indeed come soon, in a fortified Belgian town called Liège.

Victory At Liège

The Schlieffen Plan called for an attack on France through the neutral country of Belgium. Standing in the way of this assault was Liège, a Belgian town with a central citadel, or fortress, surrounded by twelve triangular forts. Twenty thousand soldiers and four hundred guns defended these forts, making Liège a formidable obstacle for the German army. On August 5, 1914, the German assault on Liège began. Ludendorff was a staff officer and therefore not directly commanding the troops. However, fierce machine gun fire drove the German attackers back, causing heavy casualties, among them the commander of the Fourteenth Infantry Brigade.

Ludendorff quickly took command of the brigade and began advancing toward the outer ring of forts. By the morning of August 6 they had advanced past the outer forts and that afternoon the citadel of Liège was in sight. But Ludendorff soon realized that his small force was alone. "It became increasingly clear," he later wrote, "that the brigade was isolated within the circle of forts, cut off from the outer world. We had to reckon with hostile attacks."[29]

Another cold night in the field, and the commander began to worry. "I was very anxious," wrote Ludendorff, "and listened feverishly for the sound of fighting. I still hoped at least one brigade had broken through the girdle of forts. But all was quiet. . . ."[30] The next morning Ludendorff's brigade began to advance once more. But this time they encountered only light enemy resistance. Thinking that another brigade had finally managed to attack the citadel, Ludendorff approached the gates and pounded on them, demanding entry to the town. Much to his surprise, when the gates opened no German troops were there, only Belgian defenders. Nevertheless, he boldly demanded their surrender. Thanks to Ludendorff's courageous actions, the citadel of Liège was soon in German hands and the Schlieffen Plan could proceed.

Almost immediately Ludendorff became a national hero. He was awarded Germany's highest military decoration, a blue, white, and gold medal called the *Pour le mérite* (For Merit). Ludendorff had shown courage and tactical skill in his first real battle. But along with these qualities, other less noble traits would appear as his military career advanced.

Meeting Hindenburg

When Paul von Hindenburg met Erich Ludendorff in the early morning hours of August 23, 1914, at the train station in Hanover, he knew nothing of Ludendorff's victory at Liège. The two made an unlikely team: Hindenburg, the old soldier from an aristocratic Prussian background, and Ludendorff, younger and from humble beginnings, ambitious and volatile. Yet this partnership would eventually be called upon to lead Germany to either glorious triumph or disgraceful defeat.

Their first assignment took Hindenburg and Ludendorff to the Eastern Front, where the German Eighth Army was retreating from Russian advances in East Prussia. Ludendorff's energy and devotion to work impressed many of the officers at Eighth Army headquarters. Lieutenant Colonel Max Hoffmann, the operations officer, wrote in his diary, "Ludendorff is a first-class fellow to work with. He is the right man for this business—ruthless and hard."[31] Hindenburg, too, noted "the intellectual powers, the almost superhuman capacity for work,"[32] of his new partner.

The two began devising a strategy to defeat the Russians. Utilizing a basic plan laid out by Colonel Hoffmann, Ludendorff massed his troops against the Russian Second Army led by General Aleksandr Samsonov. On August 26, 1914, the Battle of Tannenberg began. Four days later Samsonov's army had been crushed, with some 30,000 Russian soldiers killed or wounded and more than 100,000 taken prisoner. Morale soared when news of the victory reached Germany. The duo of Hindenburg and Ludendorff were the heroes of the Battle of Tannenberg in the eyes of the German people. Many thought that with such a great team leading the army, surely Germany would be the ultimate victor in the war.

Many Germans were certain that Germany would win the war with Paul von Hindenburg (pictured) and Erich Ludendorff leading the army.

From East to West

More victories followed on the Eastern Front as Ludendorff organized assaults against the Russian army and Hindenburg approved the plans. Each new success confirmed Ludendorff's talent as a master tactician. Yet even in victory, Ludendorff's abrasive personality came through. He gloated in his triumphs over his Russian adversaries and blamed others when things went wrong. With the gentlemanly Hindenburg receiving most of the public acclaim, Ludendorff's uneven temperament went unnoticed by the German people.

While Hindenburg and Ludendorff were demolishing the Russians on the Eastern Front, things were not going as well in the west. Chief of the German General Staff Erich von Falkenhayn believed that he could "bleed France dry" by attacking a place that the French would defend at all costs. He chose the fortress city of Verdun as his target. But Falkenhayn's assault, be-

gun in February 1916, turned into a bloody, five-month stalemate costing more than 400,000 German casualties. In the end the city did not fall, but General von Falkenhayn's career did.

On August 29, 1916, Hindenburg replaced Falkenhayn as chief of the General Staff and Ludendorff acquired the title of

A French soldier is shot near Verdun, France, as the Germans attack during a five-month-long battle.

second chief. Rejecting that title as giving him secondary status, Ludendorff instead took the designation first quartermaster-general. "In my opinion," Ludendorff later wrote, "there could be only one Chief of the General Staff; but in any case, I had been expressly assured that I should have joint responsibility in all decisions and measures that might be taken."[33] Joint responsibility, perhaps, but it was Ludendorff who made the decisions. As Colonel Hoffmann wrote in 1915, "[Hindenburg] no longer has the slightest interest in military matters; Ludendorff does everything himself."[34] Indeed, for the next two years, Ludendorff would bear responsibility for the fate of Germany.

War in the West

The Western Front was as different from the Eastern Front as the moon is from the earth. And with its barren terrain blasted clear of trees and other natural features, the ground pockmarked by craters from countless artillery shells, the Western Front could have been a lunar landscape. This was the land of trench warfare, a war of men hiding in trenches, fighting not only the enemy but also mud, rats, and constant fear. For Erich Ludendorff, who had fought fast-moving, highly mobile campaigns against the Russians, this was clearly not the way to win a war. Ludendorff's assessment of the German position in the west was that "The outlook for the coming year was exceedingly grave."[35] So, he began to plan the strategy for the coming year.

German commanders knew that the Allies were planning a massive assault in 1917. In a bold and controversial move, Ludendorff withdrew his troops from the area of the expected attack, falling back to a defensive position known as the Siegfried Line. On April 9 the Allied assault began. Ludendorff worked himself into a state of near panic as initial reports showed the Germans sustaining heavy losses. It took the even-tempered Hindenburg to calm his partner. "We have lived through more critical times than today together."[36] In the end, however, Ludendorff's plan succeeded. The Allied offensive was crushed, sending the French army into mutinous disarray.

U-boats and Politics

By 1917 Germany was being strangled by a British sea blockade. German morale plunged as war materials became scarce and food shortages caused citizens to go hungry. To Ludendorff the solution was simple: unrestricted U-boat warfare against the blockade. But this was not simply a military matter. Sinking unarmed merchant ships (as opposed to warships) would have serious political consequences. Nevertheless, Ludendorff announced on January 31, 1917, that Allied merchant ships would be sunk without warning. It didn't take long before the folly of this decision became clear. As a result, on April 6 the United States declared war on Germany. By playing politics without knowledge or experience, Erich Ludendorff had just sealed Germany's fate.

A Helping Hand to Revolution

By 1917, Russia, Germany's enemy on the Eastern Front, was quickly descending into chaos. Ammunition and food for frontline troops had become scarce or nonexistent, and many Russian soldiers lacked adequate clothing and shoes. Things were no better at home, where Russian housewives rioted to receive what little food was available and workers staged strikes against the government. For Erich Ludendorff this unrest meant the possibility of total collapse, thereby removing Russia from the war. He hoped that he could somehow help the situation along.

The opportunity soon came in the person of a secret agent code-named Parvus. Parvus was really a Russian named Alexander Helphand, who was working as a spy for Germany. He told Ludendorff that if Vladimir Lenin, leader of the Russian radicals, could return to Russia from his exile in Switzerland, it might hasten a revolution. Lu-

dendorff quickly made the arrangements. On April 9, 1917, a sealed train departed Bern, Switzerland, carrying its special passenger, Vladimir Lenin. Soon Lenin was speeding across the German countryside, heading toward the Russian capital of Petrograd (now St. Petersburg).

Upon his arrival, Lenin immediately began working to overthrow Russia's provisional government. By November 1917 the revolution was complete, with Lenin becoming the head of the new government. On March 3, 1918, Russia signed the Treaty of Brest-Litovsk, officially ending the country's participation in World War I. In his book *Tormented Warrior*, Roger Parkinson reveals Ludendorff's reaction: "How often had I not hoped for a revolution in Russia in order that our military burden might be alleviated! . . . Now it had come true. . . . I felt as though a weight had been removed from my chest."

Ludendorff and Hindenburg were now the political as well as military leaders of Germany. And they were not hesitant in using their power. German Chancellor Theobald Bethmann-Hollweg angered the duo by opposing unrestricted submarine warfare and advocating a peace resolution. By threatening to resign, Ludendorff and Hindenburg forced the chancellor to give up his office. Ludendorff also made political decisions concerning domestic affairs and even the Russian Revolution. By combining political power with military might, Ludendorff was able to put into action his theory of "total war": that an entire nation, not just the military, waged war. Now he was ready to begin preparations for the final assault that would win the war for Germany.

The Final Thrust

In preparing for the spring offensive of 1918, Ludendorff had a new, complicating factor to consider: American soldiers. Every day more and more American troops were arriving in France. Although inexperienced in battle, these soldiers were fresh and ready to fight, just what the Allies needed to bolster their exhausted armies. Ludendorff would have to strike quickly, before the Americans could effectively enter the conflict.

Operation Michael was Ludendorff's plan to attack a section of the front that was only lightly defended by British soldiers. To maintain secrecy, Ludendorff deployed his troops under the cover of darkness. Yet even as his plans were moving forward, the first quartermaster-general was beginning to show signs of the stress of command. When asked what the goal of the operation was, Ludendorff snapped: "We'll just blow a hole in the middle. The rest will follow of its own accord."[37]

With a thundering artillery barrage, Operation Michael began on March 21, 1918. At first the German assault was successful, pushing some thirty miles into enemy territory. But by April 5 Ludendorff's exhausted troops could go no further and the operation stalled. Four days later another offensive, Operation George, was launched, but by April 29 this, too, had failed. In all the two assaults had cost Germany nearly 350,000 casualties. Despite such appalling losses, Ludendorff still felt the war could be won.

Over the next two months Ludendorff tried three more offensives. But continuing supply problems, reduced troop strength, and the increasing presence of American soldiers combined to put an end to Germany's dream of victory. For Erich Ludendorff, a personal nightmare was just beginning.

Fall from Power

On July 19, 1918, Ludendorff and Hindenburg were having dinner with their staff officers, discussing the latest German defeats. When Hindenburg suggested a simple solution to the situation, Ludendorff lost control, abruptly taking over the conversation and rudely contradicting his commanding officer. A similar incident occurred later

that evening. As a staff officer recalled, "General Ludendorff straightened up from the map and, with an expression of rage on his face, turned towards the door, letting out one or two words like 'madness!' in profound irritation."[38] Clearly the war was taking a toll on Ludendorff. He admitted that he had become superstitious, relating how he had found in an old German prayer book bad omens for July 15, the day of his last, failed offensive.

On August 8, 1918, Allied infantry, supported by an artillery barrage and more than four hundred tanks, crashed through the German lines. Ludendorff called it "the black day of the German army."[39] The Allies advanced steadily for the next seven weeks, and on September 28 they reached the Siegfried Line. That night Ludendorff told Hindenburg that an immediate armistice must be arranged. By late October, however, Ludendorff reversed himself, convinced that he could regroup his army and somehow continue fighting. With the support of the German people, Ludendorff said, "The war can be maintained for some months. A fortress that surrenders without defending itself to the last is dishonored."[40] But it was too late. On October 26, 1918, Kaiser Wilhelm summoned the duo to the palace. In a tense meeting Ludendorff, finally convinced that the government would not continue the war, angrily resigned his command. Hindenburg also offered to resign but was refused; the popular field marshal had become an important symbol of German unity.

These bones collected after the five-month-long Battle of Verdun show the appalling number of casualties during World War I.

Exile and Return

Germany needed a scapegoat for losing the war and found one in Erich Ludendorff. Disturbed by increasing public hostility toward him, Ludendorff fled in disguise to Sweden in November 1918. There he wrote his memoirs, a two-volume work entitled *My War Memories,* in which he attempted to salvage his, and his army's, honor. By early 1919 Ludendorff had returned to Germany and soon entered politics. He participated in an unsuccessful attempt to overthrow the Ger-

man government in 1920. Three years later he joined a similar attempt in Munich. This plot also failed, but the name of its leader, Adolf Hitler, would not soon be forgotten.

Increasingly Ludendorff retreated into the world of occult religion. He divorced Margarethe and in September 1926 married Mathilde von Kemnitz, a doctor whose views complemented Ludendorff's own increasingly fanatical thoughts. Together they wrote books and pamphlets describing the supposed evil influence of Jews, Catholics, and Freemasons on German society. But not all of Ludendorff's writings were occult in nature. In 1936 he published *Total War,* an explanation of his theory that modern war involved the whole of a nation. In a few years World War II would prove the correctness of Ludendorff's theory.

However, it was a war that he would not live to see. Ludendorff died on December 20, 1937. During the funeral procession Adolf Hitler walked behind Ludendorff's casket, which was draped with a swastika, the symbol of Hitler's Germany. Before long the whole world would come to know that symbol as a mark of absolute evil. Old soldiers would remember Erich Ludendorff as a brilliant tactician and soldier of tremendous energy. For most, however, Ludendorff's legacy would be forever dimmed by the erratic personality that finally trapped him in a lonely world of fantasy and hate.

Chapter 3

Philippe Pétain: Hero of Verdun

It wasn't much of a road, really, just a narrow dirt lane not more than seven yards wide. Before the war, fruit farmers used it to carry their produce from the French town of Bar-le-Duc to the fortress city of Verdun on the Meuse River. But now, in early 1916, Verdun was under siege by the Germans. The little road had suddenly become a vital lifeline for the French, for it was the only road into the besieged city. An indication of its significance was the new name given to the narrow path. Henceforth the Bar-le-Duc to Verdun road would be known as *La Voie Sacrée:* the Sacred Way.

About eleven miles from Verdun the Sacred Way passed the town of Souilly. On the steps of the town hall stood a man in a French general's uniform. Tall, with steely blue eyes and a ramrod-straight posture, the general silently watched as French troops marched by. These poilus were traveling in both directions, some toward Verdun to fight the Germans, others in the opposite direction toward rest areas near Bar-le-Duc. It was a sight the sixty-year-old general would not soon forget. "My heart lurched as I saw our young men of twenty going into the furnace of Verdun . . . how saddening it was when they came back, either on their own as wounded or stragglers, or in the ranks of companies decimated by loss! Their stares seemed to be fixed in a vision of unbelievable terror . . . they drooped beneath the weight of their horrifying memories."[41]

In these words we find the measure of the man, the compassion he felt for the lives of the soldiers under his command. More than any other World War I general, Philippe Pétain saw that the old tactics of massive frontal assaults did little but waste lives in this, the first modern war. His defense of Verdun and deft handling of mutinous soldiers made him France's foremost military leader at the end of World War I. Although he has been called everything from a hero to a traitor, General Pétain never squandered the lives of the young men fighting to save France.

Cross or Sword

The birthplace of the future Hero of Verdun was the small farming town of Cauchy-à-la-Tour in northern France. There Henri Philippe Benoni Omer Pétain was born on April 24, 1856, into a family of peasant farmers. Philippe (as he preferred to be called) was the third child of Omer-Venant Pétain and his wife Clotilde. After bearing a fourth child, his mother died in 1857. Philippe was three years old when his father remarried, and by 1862 three more children had joined the Pétain family.

Philippe's stepmother paid little attention to the children of her husband's first marriage, and before long he went to live with his grandparents. At age eleven Philippe entered the Collège Saint Bertin, a religious school that prepared young men for the military. An uncle, Jean-Baptiste Legrand, who formerly taught at the school, paved the way for Philippe's entrance. Later the elderly uncle would remark that he wished "that my family will always possess men who bear the cross or the sword."[42] After eight years at Saint Bertin and two years at the Imperial Special Military School at Saint-Cyr, Philippe received his commission as an officer in 1878. Second Lieutenant Philippe Pétain was on his way to fulfill his uncle's wish.

General Philippe Pétain felt great compassion for his men and thought that frontal assault tactics did nothing but waste lives.

Slow Advancement

For French officers in peacetime, promotions came slowly. Many tried to speed their advancement by serving in one of the exotic French colonies: in Morocco, or Indochina, or perhaps Madagascar. But Pétain would remain in France for most of his military career and thus was promoted slowly. As he later remarked, "I was old as a lieutenant, as a captain, as a colonel. I have been old in all my ranks."[43]

To his colleagues and superiors, Pétain gave the impression of being businesslike but distant and aloof. The word "cold" is most often used to describe him. One evaluation called Pétain, "Silent, cold, calm, hostile to hasty judgments and always working methodically."[44] Another compared him to "a marble statue."[45] But behind this glacial exterior Pétain had an ironic sense of humor and an appreciation for the opposite sex. Although he remained a bachelor until after the war, Pétain had numerous mistresses and never missed an opportunity to flirt with a pretty young woman.

After commanding several light infantry units and serving as a staff officer in Marseille and Paris, in 1901, Pétain was assigned to teach at the École de Guerre, or War College. A major at forty-five years old, Pétain was a career soldier who had never heard a shot fired in anger. But he had not served all those years in the army without forming his own ideas of how wars should be fought.

French military tactics in the late nineteenth century were based on the concept of the direct frontal assault. Lines of troops wearing brightly colored uniforms would advance toward the enemy in the open, with bands playing and bayonets glinting in the sun. To seek cover from enemy fire was unthinkable. Marksmanship was nothing, the will to win, everything. It was grand, it was heroic, and against such modern weapons as the machine gun it was suicidal. Pétain was appalled at the waste of human lives in these assaults known as *attaque à outrance,* or "attack to the utmost." The infantry, he taught, must conquer the battlefield through individual shooting accuracy. Pétain also believed that artillery should support infantry advances rather than simply firing blindly at unseen targets. And, when properly coordinated, defensive firepower should stop enemy assaults. In short, Pétain declared, "*Le feu tue*":[46] firepower kills.

Opposition

Many in the French War Ministry were outraged by Pétain's radical theories, and his advancement slowed even further. Once he was transferred to a remote outpost, only later to be recalled to the college. During this exile, Pétain wrote, "The War College is asking for me again, but I have a bad press at the Ministry, and don't know who will win: bets are open."[47] But Pétain was popular among the students and his lectures were always filled to capacity. Even the head of the college praised him: "Of a nobility of sentiments . . . a just sense of tactics and a deep knowledge of his field, Pétain carries out a program at the school which is first

Pétain believed that artillery such as this rotating cannon should support infantry advances rather than be blindly fired at unseen targets.

class from every point of view."[48] These were the words of General Ferdinand Foch, a traditional military man who would clash with Pétain during the war.

Despite opposition, some of Pétain's theories seemed to take hold. In 1904 new army regulations incorporated his ideas of coordinating the artillery with the infantry and the use of flexible troop formations. By 1914, however, the old school of thought had reasserted itself. But Philippe Pétain was preparing to retire, an obscure fifty-eight-year-old colonel who had never seen combat, had never left France, and whose uniform bore no decorations attest-

ing to a remarkable military career. In August 1914 the guns of the German army would change Philippe Pétain's retirement plans and thrust him squarely into the jaws of the Great War.

German Offensive

At the outset of World War I, Colonel Philippe Pétain was in command of an infantry brigade in northern France. On August 4, 1914, Germany launched its

Schlieffen Plan, a grand offensive designed to conquer France by sweeping through neutral Belgium. As part of the French Fifth Army, Pétain's brigade rushed to Belgium to help stem the tide of advancing enemy soldiers. But the German onslaught was too powerful, and soon the French army was in full retreat. Pétain's concern for his troops was evident in the fact that his brigade sustained fewer losses than those around him. Yet this was war, and he could deal sternly with his men when necessary. On long nighttime marches fatigue became a problem. "From three o'clock onwards," Pétain noted in his journal, "groups of men begin not getting up after halts, and one is obliged to strike them to make them get up."[49]

While the northern retreat continued, French troops in the south were boldly advancing against the Germans just as the old style of combat decreed. The results were disastrous. German machine guns mowed down line after line of French soldiers, making August 1914 one of the bloodiest months of the entire war. It was becoming clear that Pétain's criticism of the old way of fighting was justified after all.

In August 1914 German machine guns mow down line after line of advancing French soldiers.

As casualties mounted and many officers were being relieved of their commands, Pétain's slow advancement in rank suddenly accelerated. On August 28 he became a brigadier general, a promotion he received with his customary irony: "I have just learned of my promotion to general. It even seems that they want to put me in command of a division. Are they already reduced to using such revolutionary measures?"[50] So swift was his promotion that Pétain did not even have the proper insignia for his uniform. At the house where he was staying, his hosts, upon learning of the promotion, cut the stars from the uniform of a long-deceased relative and sewed them onto the new general's uniform.

Action on the Western Front

In the months to come, General Pétain would see further action, notably at the Battle of the Marne where the Allies halted the German advance. By October 1914 Pétain was a lieutenant general in command of the Thirty-third Army Corps. As the war's first winter set in, Pétain kept his unit's morale high by arranging for leaves, establishing the army's first theater, and by personally visiting the frontline troops. By this time, however, the face of war had changed. "The glorious epoch was over," Pétain later wrote, "in which combatants had dared to face each other openly. . . . From this moment onward, war was to change in character. . . . Artillery and machine guns were to become masters of the field of battle."[51]

Trench warfare had begun, something that even Pétain had not foreseen.

May 9, 1915, saw yet another attack by the French, this time in the Artois region. Pétain again skillfully planned the use of his artillery. "There will be a sufficient number of guns," Pétain told his men, "to ensure your attack is a success. Let us first crush the enemy by artillery fire and afterward we shall win our victory."[52] He was always quick to expend ammunition rather than lives. While other commanders felt that five thousand hand grenades per corps would be enough, Pétain exclaimed, "I want fifty thousand."[53] Pétain's Thirty-third Corps broke through the German lines and advanced more than two miles into enemy territory, the only one of five corps to do so. But it was only a temporary victory. Without sufficient reserves to sustain the thrust, the offensive ultimately failed. The Artois offensive cost France nearly fifty thousand men. Pétain blamed his superiors, calling them madmen. "Foch," he angrily complained, "tells us to attack, without caring about the state of preparation."[54]

Manpower, Pétain felt, should be conserved for the day when the Germans would make their final assault. In early 1916 it appeared that Germany was ready to do just that, at an ancient fortress city called Verdun.

Verdun

The Germans had a code name for their invasion plan: *Gericht*, which can be translated

An Ancient Fortress City

For two thousand years Verdun has been an important city, a fortress standing ready to repel foreign invaders. In 843 the Treaty of Verdun partitioned Emperor Charlemagne's dominion into three kingdoms, Western Frankish (French) and Eastern Frankish (German), with Verdun in a middle kingdom called Lotharingia. A natural rivalry between the French and Germans for the middle territory inevitably arose.

After being under German rule since the tenth century, Verdun was seized by King Henry II of France in 1552. Verdun suffered many sieges throughout its history, including a devastating assault by the Prussians in 1792. The Franco-Prussian War of 1870–71 brought control of Verdun back to Germany until 1873. The loss of the Alsace-Lorraine region to Germany in the Franco-Prussian War prompted France to improve Verdun's fortifications in preparation for a future attack from Germany.

General Philippe Pétain well understood the importance of Verdun. As quoted in Richard Griffiths's book *Pétain: A Biography of Marshal Philippe Pétain of Vichy*, in June 1916, Pétain wrote, "Verdun is menaced and Verdun must not fall. The capture of this city would constitute for the Germans an inestimable success which would greatly raise their morale and correspondingly lower our own." Philippe Pétain denied Germany that "inestimable success" and in doing so became the Hero of Verdun.

as "the execution place." What German Chief of Staff Erich von Falkenhayn wanted was a target that the French would defend at all costs. In doing so, the French army would either "bleed itself white" defending the place or, if defeated, cause severe damage to French morale. That place was Verdun.

The German attack began with a massive artillery barrage before dawn on February 21, 1916. Four days later the massive fortress called Fort Douaumont, which Pétain later called the cornerstone of the Verdun defenses, fell to the Germans. That same day Pétain received word that he was to take command of Verdun's defense. The general who had advocated a strong defense was now in charge of defending France's great symbol of national freedom.

His first job was to assure that the supply line to Verdun remained open. That meant keeping traffic on the Bar-le-Duc to Verdun road—the Sacred Way—moving. Although suffering from double pneumonia, Pétain immediately took control. He decreed that the road was to be used by vehicles only; troops would march along the sides. Any truck that broke down was to be immediately pushed off the road and fixed later by repair crews. Pétain deployed thousands of older reserve troops known as territorials along the sides of the road. Armed only with shovels and determination, the territorials kept the road passable, filling holes and cracks with crushed rock twenty-four hours a day.

Pétain's skill at organization paid off. In the first week some 190,000 men and 25,000 tons of ammunition and equipment traveled over the Sacred Way. By June a truck was passing by every fourteen seconds, rolling up enough mileage to circle the earth twenty-five times. By assuring a continual flow of supplies, by rotating fresh troops to the front, and by skillful defensive use of artillery, Pétain was able to stall the German offensive. The defenders of Verdun adopted the motto *"Ils ne passeront pas!"*: They shall not pass! Unfortunately, saving Verdun wasn't enough to please Pétain's superiors.

During the siege of Verdun, Pétain had concentrated on defense, to the growing concern of his superiors. In the two months he had been at Verdun he had taken no offensive action, and General Foch feared that Pétain was becoming too cautious. So, on April 19, 1916, Pétain was given command of Army Group Center while the more aggressive General Robert Nivelle took over at Verdun. For Pétain it was a promotion and the opportunity to lead an even larger force. Yet he knew it was a move to distance him from the city he had saved. "You see in me," Pétain told a friend, "a general who has just been relieved of his command."[55]

In July 1916 the British began their offensive along the Somme River (mentioned in the introduction), relieving some pressure from the defenders at Verdun. By December,

French soldiers stand outside a bunker at Verdun, France. General Pétain focused on defensive measures at Verdun, which concerned his superiors.

Nivelle had retaken most of the ground gained by the German offensives. Buoyed by his victories and a subsequent promotion to commander in chief, Nivelle felt that he was now prepared to achieve the breakthrough that would finally win the war for the Allies. What he didn't count on was the mounting psychological toll the war was taking on the soldiers in the trenches.

Mutiny!

Nivelle began a bold assault in the spring of 1917, a "giant fist" to smash the German army. But French secrecy was lax and the Germans knew the attack was coming. Under intense German machine gunfire, French casualties numbered more than one hundred thousand in the first three weeks of the offensive. Such appalling losses finally proved too much for the surviving French poilus. Many soldiers simply sat in the trenches, refusing to fight. Slogans such as "Down with the war!" and "Death to those responsible!" began to appear. Every day thousands more French soldiers joined the rebellion; by June 1917 more than half of the French army was affected.

In the midst of the mutinies, on May 15, 1917, Philippe Pétain became commander in chief of the French armies, replacing a disgraced Nivelle. If Pétain was compassionate with his troops in battle, he could also be tough when the situation demanded. He ordered that leaders of the mutinies be executed, although out of more than four hundred who received the death sentence, only fifty-five were actually executed. For the ordinary soldier, exhausted and discouraged by three years of war, Pétain promised improved conditions including better food, more rest periods behind the lines, and better medical facilities. Pétain personally visited many frontline units and promised to end the wasting of lives in useless offensives, saying "We must wait for the Americans and the tanks."[56]

By the end of June the worst of the mutinies had been suppressed and morale was

A Crisis of Morale

During the mutinies of 1917 the French army as well as the nation as a whole came close to crumbling. Only tight secrecy kept Germany from learning about and exploiting this grave crisis. In his first official report on the mutinies, quoted in Correlli Barnett's book *The Swordbearers,* Philippe Pétain reveals his understanding of the pressures facing those on the front lines:

All that period of orders and counter-orders which followed till the end of the month has been disastrous. The troops put in the line on April 19 received successively information that they would attack on the 23rd, then the 25th, then the 29th, at last May 3 and 5. Successive counter-orders of this kind are depressing in the extreme for those carrying them out. To prepare to attack is to face the probability of death. One deliberately accepts this idea once. But when they see the awful moment postponed again and again the bravest and the steadiest become demoralized. In the end, physical resistance and nervous tension alike have their limits. The troops who attacked on May 5 were at the end of their tether, having been on the front line for seventeen days under intense and continuous fire.

on an upswing. As at Verdun, Pétain had once more overcome a national crisis. Now, with American troops arriving in Europe, the newly appointed commander in chief could lead the French army to the final victory.

End of the War

To further encourage his army, Pétain began staging a series of limited offensives in late 1917. Victories in these operations prepared French forces for the German offensive that was anticipated for the next spring. On March 21, 1918, the expected German assault began with a massive artillery barrage followed by attacking storm troopers. At first the Germans advanced rapidly, but they were soon slowed by British, French, and American soldiers. Pétain encouraged his troops: "If we can hold on until the end of June, our situation will be excellent. In July we can resume the offensive; after that, victory will be ours."[57]

Victory would indeed belong to the Allies, but not without dissension among the ranks. Like his American colleague, General John J. "Black Jack" Pershing, Pétain wanted a decisive victory over the German army. But Marshal Ferdinand Foch, commander of all Allied forces, pushed for an armistice that would spare further bloodshed. As Pétain would later recall: "Neither Pershing nor I wanted the Armistice. . . . It

People fill the streets of Paris, France, on November 11, 1918, to celebrate the end of the war.

is easy to prove to the German people that they have not been beaten. I only hope that that does not lead us to a second World War even more terrible than the first. On the evening of the armistice, I wept."[58] But the world had had its fill of war, violence, and senseless death. On November 11, 1918, the guns fell silent on the Western Front. The war was over.

Marshal of France

If the account of Philippe Pétain's life were to end here, it would be the inspiring story of an obscure army officer nearing retirement who heeded his country's call and in the process became a national hero. But in his later years, circumstances that no one could foresee in 1918 would tarnish the luster of the Hero of Verdun.

After the war, Pétain was appointed a marshal of France. He served on France's Supreme War Council and was the army's inspector general until his retirement in 1931 at age seventy-five. Ever mindful of the possibility of a renewed German threat, Pétain masterminded the construction of the Maginot Line, a line of heavy fortifications running along France's border with Ger-many. But this static defense system was no match for Germany's highly mobile army. In 1940 German tanks simply went around the Maginot Line in a massive assault against France. The Second World War, the one that Pétain had feared would result from an easy armistice, had come to France.

Philippe Pétain (left) maintained that he cooperated with Hitler (right) and the Nazi regime in order to protect France. In August 1945 Pétain was found guilty of treason.

Believing that Germany would soon dominate all of Europe, Pétain became the head of a new French government with its capital at the city of Vichy. He cooperated with the Nazi regime, bringing charges of disloyalty upon himself after the war. Pétain maintained that he was only cooperating in order to protect France from further destruction. But on August 15, 1945, eighty-nine-year-old Philippe Pétain, now nearly deaf, was found guilty of treason and sentenced to death. Two days later the sentence was commuted to life in prison.

Philippe Pétain spent the last years of his life in an old fortress that served as his prison on the Ile d'Yeu, a tiny island eleven miles off the western coast of France. He died there of respiratory failure on July 23, 1951. Was Pétain a hero or a traitor? Did he save France in the First World War only to give it to the Germans in the second? The controversy lives on half a century after his death. But no one can dispute Philippe Pétain's role as the Hero of Verdun, his decisive handling of the mutinies, or his constant concern for the morale and saftey of his troops. For years after World War I Petain was the symbol of France's victory, and he continued to show a great devotion to his country and to his duty. Unfortunately, it was that same devotion that caused him to make the decisions that tarnished his reputation. In a 1945 letter, Pétain wrote, "At my age, one only fears one thing: not to have done all one's duty."[59] Whatever the verdict of history, Marshal Philippe Pétain did his duty as he saw it.

Chapter 4

William "Billy" Mitchell: Prophet of Airpower

At the beginning of the twentieth century few frontiers on the North American continent remained unexplored. One remote territory, however, still held a lure for adventurers and explorers, prospectors and swindlers—the frozen reaches of Alaska. This barely explored wilderness was also of interest to the U.S. Army, which recognized Alaska's strategic value as America's farthest outpost on the Pacific Ocean. The job of connecting Alaska to the United States via telegraph lines fell to the Army Signal Corps.

A twenty-one-year-old lieutenant named William Mitchell was placed in charge of the army's project of stringing telegraph lines across the Alaskan wilderness. "Alaska—how far it sounds!"[60] he would later write. And for that very reason the adventurous lieutenant had requested the assignment. He handled the job with a confidence that belied his youth. And in the dead of the Alaskan winter when no work could be done, Mitchell remained in a log cabin studying Signal Corps manuals. He learned about electricity, wireless telegraphy, photography, and especially a new discipline called aeronautics.

Years later, as World War I raged in Europe, Billy Mitchell would use his knowledge of aeronautics to create an American air force. He developed aerial combat strategies that helped the Allies ultimately triumph over Germany. But perhaps his greatest achievement was his vision of what an air force *should* be, and his courage to promote that vision regardless of personal cost.

Did Mitchell's reading of aeronautical subjects in the long Alaskan nights strike a spark that would eventually ignite his brilliant aviation career and, ultimately, his downfall? While it will never be known for sure, no one can doubt that General William "Billy" Mitchell became an outspoken prophet for airpower, only to have his cries lost in a wilderness of indifference as big as the Alaskan outdoors.

An Idyllic Childhood

Billy Mitchell was born into a well-to-do Wisconsin family. His grandfather had emigrated from Scotland to become a wealthy banker and railroad magnate in Milwaukee. John Lendrum Mitchell, Billy's father, was more interested in politics and the arts than in business and had studied at the finest European schools. It was while his parents were on an extended tour of Europe that William Mitchell was born in Nice, France, on December 29, 1879. The Mitchells spent three years in France before returning home to Meadowmere, the four-hundred-acre family estate near Milwaukee.

For Willy, as he was known to the family, Meadowmere was an ideal place for an active youngster to grow up. As one of Willy's playmates later wrote, there were "ponies to ride, cows to milk, a private race course, a private lake quite large enough to play Corsair upon in a flat-bottomed rowboat which leaked—with Willy, of course, as Pirate Chief."[61] Willy became proficient with a rifle and enjoyed the outdoors, hunting and camping in the woods around Meadowmere.

Willy's mother, Harriet Mitchell, was a woman of "force and dignity,"[62] and had perhaps the most influence during Willy's formative years. Once when Willy became frustrated trying to ride a particularly cantankerous pony, he complained, "Mummy, I can't handle that nasty beast."[63] His mother gently counseled her son to "go on riding it until you can."[64]

Pictured here in 1917 is Air Service commander William "Billy" Mitchell.

Education

Willy's education was typical of a privileged youth in the late nineteenth century. After attending private school in Milwaukee, he entered Racine College, an Episcopal preparatory school, in 1889 at age ten. Naturally more interested in sports than academics, Willy played baseball and polo. His grades were merely adequate and he had his share of negative disciplinary reports, which included such violations as "talking before grace in the dining room, boisterous conduct at table, disorder in dormitory, and offenses of that kind."[65] He was, in short, a typical schoolboy.

In 1895, after six years at Racine College, Billy Mitchell was admitted to Columbian College (known today as George Washington University) in Washington, D.C. As an almost-sixteen-year-old freshman, Billy was the

Seeking adventure, Mitchell enlisted in the army when the United States declared war on Spain after the USS Maine *exploded in Havana, Cuba.*

youngest student at the college. He impressed his classmates, not with his academic skills, but with the latest sports equipment—golf clubs, tennis racquets, fishing gear, and guns.

But Billy Mitchell's education went beyond the classroom. American history became a passion for him, and a heightened patriotism developed due perhaps to his foreign birth. "America," recalled his sister Ruth, "its inspiring past and glowing future, became the very warp and woof of Bill's own mind."[66] Tours of European and American battlefields with his father, who was by then a U.S. senator, fueled in him an abiding interest in military history. Although he was not yet thinking of a military career, his thirst for adventure would soon lead Billy Mitchell in that direction.

Soldier Boy

On February 15, 1898, the U.S. battleship *Maine* exploded in Havana harbor; two months later the Spanish-American War be-

gan. Sitting in the Senate gallery as the declaration of war was passed, Billy Mitchell saw his chance to trade college routine for some adventure. Although still a junior at Columbian College, the eighteen-year-old rushed to enlist in the First Wisconsin Volunteer Regiment. Soon Private Billy Mitchell was boarding a train for Florida, anticipating action in Cuba. A family friend watched Billy depart and wrote his mother, "I soon recognized him by a certain swing to his walk and the extreme badness of his hat—it was the very worst hat I ever saw. He gave us a shy little jerk of his hand in response to our frantic wavings. . . . Then we left him . . . a typical soldier boy off to the wars."[67]

Within a week Private Billy Mitchell had become Second Lieutenant Billy Mitchell of the U.S. Army Signal Corps. As the youngest officer in the army, Billy realized the advantages of having a senator for a father. "Influence," he wrote, "cuts a larger figure in this war than merit."[68] His hopes of seeing action were dashed when Spain sued for peace before his regiment could mobilize. But he didn't let this setback discourage him. "I'm going to get there some way or another," he wrote his father. "I've been waiting all summer to get a chance to do something and have not had it, and think it would be a shame to go home now."[69] His perseverance paid off, and in December 1898, Billy Mitchell sailed for Cuba.

In 1899 Lieutenant Mitchell supervised the stringing of telephone wires in Cuba. His regiment constructed more miles of wire than any other unit.

Signal Corps Officer

As a lieutenant in the Signal Corps, Mitchell supervised the stringing of telegraph wires for the army of occupation. His regiment constructed 138 miles of wire, more than any other unit in Cuba. His commanding officer commended Mitchell, noting in an official report that "this officer, despite his youth, is a man of ability, energy and intelligence."[70] When an insurrection led by rebel general Emilio Aguinaldo broke out in the Philippines, Mitchell applied for a transfer. In October 1899 his orders came through and Mitchell headed for action in the far Pacific.

Once again, Mitchell set about constructing telegraph lines. Having limited supplies, he had to use all his imagination and resourcefulness, making telegraph cable from barbed wire fences and insulators from broken bottles. With such primitive materials Mitchell laid seventy-five miles of telegraph line through enemy infested countryside. In addition, his regiment broke up several bands of insurgents and even captured Aguinaldo's second in command.

Then Mitchell contracted malaria, and while recovering he thought about leaving the army. But soon adventure was calling once more, and Billy Mitchell headed to another remote part of the world: Alaska.

A Natural Sort of Soldier

Mitchell spent the next two years constructing a telegraph line that spanned seventeen hundred miles of Alaska's icy wilderness. When weather conditions got so bad that work was impossible, Mitchell holed up in an isolated cabin with his friend Dutch De-Haus, poring over Signal Corps manuals in preparation for his captaincy exam. Before returning to the United States in 1903 he passed the exam, making him, at age twenty-three, the youngest captain in the army. He also experienced a personal milestone with his marriage to Caroline Stoddard in December of that year. It was the first of two marriages for Billy Mitchell.

By the time he returned to the United States the army had expanded to a force some one hundred thousand strong. Mitchell, an athletically built young man with

intense brown eyes and a cleft chin, now realized that military service would be his career. "I am naturally a sort of soldier," he wrote his father. "I like the service, I like to have my command, and I like service in the field."[71] For the next nine years Billy Mitchell held various assignments, which included restoring telegraph lines to San Francisco in the wake of that city's devastating 1906 earthquake. He returned to the Philippines in 1909 to conduct undercover investigations of military activity—especially Japan's—in the Pacific.

On the General Staff

In February 1913 Mitchell joined the General Staff in Washington, D.C., where his main duty involved analyzing intelligence reports from Europe. As he watched Europe gradually slide toward war, he became an outspoken critic of America's lack of military preparedness. In a 1915 report entitled "Our Faulty Military Policy," he criticized America's readiness for war. "The military policy of the United States," Mitchell wrote, "is and has been to prepare for war *after such war has actually broken out.*"[72] Such caustic comments would continue throughout Mitchell's career, with devastating results.

Despite his outspoken personality, Mitchell was one of the most promising officers on the General Staff and, at age thirty-three, the youngest. As an intelligence analyst he studied the early development of aviation in the Balkan Wars of 1912–13. Soon Mitchell was appointed head of the

Signal Corps' Aviation Section. He immediately began a campaign to recruit young men for flight training. Since no military aviation training facilities existed, Mitchell contracted with civilian flight schools to train these recruits. His goal was to produce five hundred pilots, the number authorized by President Woodrow Wilson.

The United States bought its first airplane from the Wright Brothers in 1909, and soon thereafter six officers became qualified pilots. Ironically, Billy Mitchell was not one of them. He began his own flight training in 1916, paying for instruction himself (a total of $1,470) because government money had not yet been appropriated. Taking lessons in his off-duty hours, the thirty-six-year-old Mitchell was a no-nonsense student. "You forget I'm an Army major," he told his instructor, "and

treat me like anyone else who's here to learn."[73] After thirty-six lessons, Mitchell had mastered the rudiments of flying.

By March 1917 Europe had been at war for almost three years. Billy Mitchell was ordered to go to France "for the specific purpose of observing the manufacture and development of aircraft."[74] As he traveled through Europe on his way to Paris, the United States declared war on Germany. America had entered World War I.

War in the Air

Upon his arrival in Paris, Mitchell immediately went to work. He set up an office, assembled a volunteer staff, and began learning

A 1908 photograph of Wilbur Wright flying his plane. The U.S. government purchased its first airplane from the Wright Brothers in 1909.

about aerial combat from French aeronautical experts. Mitchell was amazed to discover that European aviation was far more advanced than in the United States. French and British pursuit pilots were tangling daily with the Germans in aerial "dogfights," while lumbering bombers dropped tons of explosives behind enemy lines. Back in America, recruits were still training in obsolete, 1914-model airplanes.

Ace of Aces

In July 1917 Billy Mitchell took an automobile tour through the northern part of France, examining areas that might be suitable for new airfields. His journey completed, he was riding through the back roads of France when his car's engine sputtered to a stop. Mitchell's chauffeur couldn't fix the engine, so a companion riding in another car, Major Townsend F. Dodd, suggested that his own chauffeur might be able to help.

The gangly young chauffeur bent over the engine, quickly diagnosed the trouble, and had the car running in just a few minutes. As Mitchell recounts in *Great Battles of World War I in the Air*, compiled by Frank C. Platt:

"That day at luncheon I asked Dodd where he obtained his chauffeur, and he replied that Lewis had got him in the United States to go along with us. He was a champion automobile racing driver, Dodd told me, and he had proved himself to be one of the best soldiers he had ever known. His name was Rickenbacker."

Edward V. "Eddie" Rickenbacker told Mitchell he wanted to become a pilot; he learned to fly in less than three weeks. As a member of the Ninety-fourth Aero Squadron, Rickenbacker became one of World War I's greatest pilots, downing twenty-six enemy aircraft to earn the title "Ace of Aces."

When Mitchell toured the Western Front two weeks after his arrival in France, he was appalled at the useless slaughter going on. "What a foolish kind of war this seemed," he wrote, "where an army could not advance twenty or thirty miles for months, even with nobody opposing them!"[75] He took more flying lessons from one of France's best pilots and soon won his wings as a junior military aviator.

Mitchell bombarded Washington with his ideas for an American air presence in Europe, typing lengthy reports late into the night. The generals back home, however, ignored Mitchell's suggestions, certain that he could not have become an expert on aerial warfare in such a short time. In addition, they were still convinced that ground campaigns would ultimately win the war.

But as Billy Mitchell flew over the Western Front, he gained a perspective on the war that no other American had. "One flight over the lines gave me a much clearer impression of how the armies were laid out than any amount of traveling around on the ground. . . . We could cross the lines of these contending armies in a few minutes in our airplane, whereas the armies had been locked in the struggle, immovable, powerless to advance, for three years."[76] It was obvious to Billy Mitchell that without control of the air, Allied ground forces would have limited effectiveness.

Into the Air

After a year of planning and preparation, Billy Mitchell was ready to send his pilots into the skies above France. The first U.S. aerial action occurred on the foggy morning of April 14, 1918, when American aviators shot down two German aircraft. It was a brief battle, as Mitchell later recalled: "Both German airplanes had been brought down and our pilots were back on the airdrome within four and one-half minutes after they left it. It was the most remarkable exhibition ever given on the Western front, and occurred in full view of all the soldiers and citizens residing in that part of the country."[77] By the end of the month American pilots were flying missions every day.

Mitchell now had an observation group and pursuit, or fighter, groups active on the Western Front. His self-confidence showed through even as he walked around the airdrome. "He didn't walk like other men," one pilot observed, "and though he was modest and considerate of everybody, there was pride in every movement. Even if he had only eight or ten feet to walk, he went at it as though he were marching a mile, and was late."[78]

When it came to discipline he was firm but fair. "Mitchell never asked his men to do anything which he would not undertake to do himself"[79] became a popular commentary on Billy Mitchell's style of command. But he needed tough self-discipline as well to cope with the dan-

In April 1918 Mitchell's pilots shot down two German aircraft in a brief aerial dogfight.

gerous nature of combat aviation. He had to bear the frequent burden of the deaths of his men, often due to accident or mechanical failure rather than combat. It was just such a failure that took the life of his twenty-three-year-old brother John on May 27, 1918.

Château-Thierry

The German army's massive spring offensive began on March 21, 1918. By July Germany was threatening to break through at Château-Thierry. There, a salient, or bulge, had formed where enemy troops had advanced furthest into the Allied lines. American and French troops struggled to hold back the German onslaught.

Billy Mitchell moved his squadrons to Château-Thierry and soon American aviators were fighting against superior numbers of German aircraft. Mitchell himself continued to fly reconnaissance missions along the front. He bravely flew alone, "because if I took several planes along with me, we would be slowed up, easily noticed and certainly brought to combat. This would have interfered with my work of watching everything and preparing ahead of time for what we should do."[80]

Mitchell's discovery of a key German supply depot led to a combined British-American bombing raid that took the enemy completely by surprise. Although outnumbered, the Americans were able to put the German aviators on the defensive for the first time in the war. Mitchell later speculated on what he could have accomplished "if we had had one thousand good airplanes instead of a measly two hundred and fifty!"[81]

On July 27, 1918, Mitchell, now a colonel, was appointed chief of the Air Service of the First Army. He immediately began preparations for the biggest air operation of the war.

Victory at St. Mihiel

In September 1918 as the German army mounted its last desperate push for victory, the Allied forces fought to reduce another

Death in the Air

With war inevitably comes death, especially for the World War I aviator. Flying a frail machine hundreds or thousands of feet in the air, death could be both swift and horrible. Parachutes were not in common use, so when an airplane was disabled by enemy fire its pilot had little hope of escaping. When an airman was shot down he was usually condemned to suffer a solitary death.

Billy Mitchell knew all too well that many of the young pilots he sent aloft would not return. In his *Memoirs of World War I,* Mitchell describes the horror of death in the air as well as admiration for his men:

We had our losses, too. . . . The burning of a pilot in the air as his ship catches fire from the hostile flaming bullets is a terrible thing. He is there alone, suspended in space, with no companion to share his misery, no man at his elbow to support him, as in the infantry on the ground. When he is wounded and falls, it is for thousands of feet, instead of two or three, as a man on the ground does. We were inflicting a loss of at least three to one on the enemy, though, which was remarkable for a new outfit. Our men were full of dash and exceptionally cool in combat.

salient, this one at the town of St. Mihiel. In support of the attack, which involved some 500,000 American and 100,000 French troops, Billy Mitchell commanded a massive force of 1,481 aircraft. Mitchell's commanding officer observed that "Colonel Mitchell had under him, composed of our own and of Allied organizations, the largest air force that had at any time been gathered together . . . on any front during the World War."[82]

Mitchell masterfully commanded his aerial armada. "I so timed the attacks," he later wrote, "that several hundred [aircraft] would hit from the right side of the salient and then several hundred would hit from the left side. As soon as the combat became general, the main attack was launched by aircraft which had flown clear around both forces and attacked the enemy in the rear."[83] With Mitchell's air force controlling the skies, American ground forces destroyed the St. Mihiel salient in two days.

General John J. Pershing wrote to Billy Mitchell after the victory at St. Mihiel, "Please accept my sincere congratulations on the successful and very important part taken by the Air Forces under your command in the first offensive of the First American Army."[84] Mitchell had demonstrated his skill in commanding a large air force and, as a result, was promoted to the rank of brigadier general. As the war staggered toward its conclusion, Mitchell continued to pursue his goal of a mighty American air force. Unfortunately, the methods he used worked against him and eventually destroyed his career.

A Hero's Return

Always thinking up radical new ideas, Billy Mitchell was working on a plan to drop twelve thousand troops by parachute behind enemy lines when the armistice intervened on November 11, 1918. When he returned to the United States in February 1919, a group of military aviators circled his ship in their planes as a salute to their chief and hero. Appointed assistant chief of the Air Service, Mitchell was eager to spread the word about airpower at home. But he was in for a great disappointment. "General Mitchell," wrote fellow aviator H. H. Arnold, "came back to a nation which was tired of war, not a fertile soil for his teachings and pleadings for air power."[85]

Mitchell envisioned an air force as a separate military branch equal to the army and navy. No longer could ground and sea forces operate effectively, he brashly explained, without adequate air support. Mitchell especially alienated navy admirals by insisting that their huge battleships were vulnerable to air attack. In 1921 he dramatically proved his point by sinking the captured German battleship *Ostfriesland* and the retired American battleship *Alabama* while a stunned group of naval officers looked on.

Although popular with the American public, Billy Mitchell's increasingly strident criticism of the military establishment won him few friends in Washington. When his term as assistant chief of the Air Service expired in 1925, he was not reappointed. As a result he lost his wartime rank of brigadier general. Once more a colonel, Mitchell was shuttled off to an obscure post near San Antonio, Texas.

Mitchell on Trial

In September 1925 the navy airship *Shenandoah* crashed in a storm, killing thirteen crewmen. Denouncing the flight as a mere publicity stunt, Mitchell once more blasted the military establishment. When asked by reporters to comment on this and another recent air crash, Mitchell said, "These accidents are the result of the incompetency, the criminal negligence, and the most treasonable negligence of our national defense by the Navy and War Departments."[86] Such open defiance by a military officer would not be tolerated, and Mitchell knew it. He also knew that, during his inevitable court-martial, he could acquaint the American public with his views on aviation.

On October 28, 1925, the court-martial of Billy Mitchell began. After seven weeks of testimony, much of which was favorable to Mitchell, he was found guilty of conduct unbecoming an officer. His sentence was five years' suspension from rank, command, and pay. President Calvin Coolidge modified the sentence, restoring Mitchell to half pay. But, unwilling to live as "an ob-

Mitchell alienated navy admirals when he demonstrated the vulnerability of U.S. battleships by sinking the retired USS Alabama *(pictured) in an air attack.*

ject of government charity,"[87] Colonel William "Billy" Mitchell resigned from the U.S. Army on February 1, 1926.

Civilian Crusader

What a soldier could not whisper with impunity a civilian could shout freely from the rooftops. And Billy Mitchell did just that, promoting his ideas for the future of aviation in scores of lectures, newspaper columns, and magazine articles. When Franklin D. Roosevelt became president in 1933 there was talk of Billy Mitchell assuming the newly created post of secretary of air. To Mitchell's dismay, the appointment never came.

On February 19, 1936, fifty-six-year-old Billy Mitchell died of heart failure. It was a cold February 22, Washington's Birthday, when he was laid to rest in the Mitchell family plot in Milwaukee. Taps was played, a salute was fired, and a wreath was laid in the name of President Roosevelt.

Since his days in the Philippines, Billy Mitchell had been concerned with Japan's military adventurism. While others looked with alarm at Nazi Germany's growing power, Mitchell gazed in the other direction, toward the Pacific. A year before his death he told a veterans group, "It is not with Europe that our greatest future concern lies. It is with the Far East."[88] Six and one-half years later Japanese aircraft filled the skies over Hawaii. Just as Mitchell's

In 1925 Mitchell (standing) was found guilty of conduct unbecoming an officer. He ultimately resigned from the U.S. Army.

planes had sunk the *Ostfriesland,* Japanese bombs sank or damaged eight battleships in Pearl Harbor. Billy Mitchell, prophet of airpower, had gotten it right all along.

Billy Mitchell's dream of a mighty U.S. Air Force as an independent military service came true in 1947. Although he did not live to see that dream become reality, his vision and determination brought airpower to the public's attention at a time when aviation was still in its infancy. His patriotism was undeniable, as was his willingness to sacrifice his career for his beliefs. The abrasive personality that ultimately led to Billy Mitchell's downfall cannot erase the passion he felt for the awesome power of flight.

Chapter 5

Douglas Haig: The Gentleman Soldier

The British Expeditionary Force (BEF) had finally arrived in France. Its mission: to support the French army against the onslaught of German forces now bashing their way through neutral Belgium. As a small army of only one hundred thousand men, the BEF was sent to the French left flank near the Belgian town of Mons, an area where little action was expected.

But the Germans came, sweeping everything before them, and soon the British were making a hasty retreat. On August 25, 1914, General Douglas Haig, commander of the British I Corps, entered the village of Landrecies where his exhausted troops halted for the night. Haig himself was suffering from a stomach disorder and needed the brief respite as much as his men. But rest would not come that night.

A German force surrounded the town, catching Haig and his soldiers off guard. Panic ensued and as enemy fire drew closer Haig hastily ordered the town barricaded in preparation for battle. "If we can't get away," Haig cried, "we will fight to the last man. If we are caught, by God, we'll sell our lives dearly."[89]

But the battle never materialized. After a brief skirmish the Germans were driven off with only a few casualties on either side. Haig's uncharacteristic moment of panic may be attributed to his illness or to the strain of retreating from a superior German force. It was the first and only time during the war that he lost his usual stolid composure. Yet it also showed that, even in a moment of impending disaster, Douglas Haig was prepared to stand fast and fight to the death for the country he loved.

Throughout World War I, Haig's successes on the battlefield were tempered by his reputation as merely a "safe" general who absorbed his losses with true British reserve. Those losses would lead some to charge that Haig was callous and stupid, sending men to their deaths in massive attacks that had little chance of succeeding.

Yet his organizational skills and leadership abilities played a large part in securing the Allied victory.

A Scottish Lad

Whiskey may have made John Haig a wealthy man, but it did not give him entrance to Scottish society. To many of his neighbors he was simply a man who had made his fortune in the distillery business. When in 1839 he married Rachel Veitch, a woman nineteen years his junior, her upper-class background gave John a certain respectability. Douglas, the youngest of their eleven children, was born on June 19, 1861, in Edinburgh, Scotland. John Haig's business as well as his poor health (due in no small part to the whiskey he both produced and consumed) kept his influence minimal during Douglas's early life. His mother was more than willing to fill that void, becoming overly solicitous of her children to compensate for her husband's neglect. The result was a spoiled young Douglas, later described by colleague and biographer John Charteris as "a small, bad-tempered, bekilted child with a crop of bright yellow curls . . . bearing in his hands a drum with the inscription, 'Douglas Haig—sometimes a good boy.'"[90]

Douglas's early endeavors at various schools reveal a boy who was inattentive and lazy. In 1875 he enrolled at Clifton College,

Some considered General Douglas Haig reserved and callous, but his leadership played a large part in securing the Allied victory.

a distinguished boarding school, where he gradually became if not a brilliant student at least an average one. But the personality traits that would mark his adult years were beginning to appear. "Already at Clifton," wrote Charteris, "he was developing that quality of 'aloneness' which was so prominent a characteristic of his later life. He was his own judge, his own taskmaster; he set the standard for himself, and he did not allow himself to be deflected a hair's breadth from his intentions or to be swayed by the opinions of others."[91]

A Gentleman at Oxford

Rachel Haig wanted her favorite son, Douglas, to have a proper British education. So in the fall of 1880, nineteen-year-old Douglas Haig entered Brasenose College, Oxford. For Douglas, Brasenose brought a sense of independence he had not known before. The social aspects of university life were as important to him, if not more so, than academic excellence. Already a skilled horseman, Douglas rode and played polo. He joined several exclusive clubs and discussed politics and religion over wine with his fellow scholars. As for his grades, they were merely average. When he left the university in 1883, he didn't receive a degree due to missing an earlier term because of illness. It never seemed to bother him. Indeed, once through with Oxford, Haig was quite able to relegate it to past history. This ability to remain emotionally detached from people and organizations would follow him throughout his life.

Oxford did, however, play an important role in developing Douglas Haig's character, for it was there he had discovered a "sense of his own importance."[92] He developed impeccable manners, was well dressed, and quietly self-confident. He felt superior to those around him but never let it show. The spoiled little boy with the yellow curls had become a gentleman, as his mother had hoped.

Sandhurst

Nowhere is it recorded exactly when Douglas Haig decided on a military career, but in January 1884 he entered the Royal Military Academy at Sandhurst. At the academy his attitude toward studies was in marked contrast to his previous academic indifference. As a fellow student noted, "Haig worked harder

Haig received a proper British education at Brasenose College in Oxford, England.

than anyone else and was seldom seen at Mess except for meals."[93] He made few friends at Sandhurst and was seen as cold and aloof by his peers.

But Haig's diligence was rewarded by his appointment as under officer, a position of honor, and by graduating first in order of merit. When asked which cadet had the most promising future, an instructor said, "A Scottish lad, Douglas Haig, is top in almost everything—books, drill, riding and sports; he is to go into the cavalry, and, before he is finished, he will be top of the Army."[94]

The Educated Soldier

As an accomplished horseman and polo player it was only natural that Douglas Haig would choose the cavalry as his military assignment. In February 1885 Lieutenant Haig joined the Seventh Hussars, an elite cavalry regiment known as the "Queen's Own." Haig looked every bit the dashing cavalryman, tall in the saddle with alert blue eyes and square jaw, his head held high. In 1886 the regiment was sent to Britain's colonial outpost of India, where Haig would spend the next seven years. His superiors were impressed with his leadership and administrative work, but were often bewildered by Haig's difficulty in spoken communication. The Seventh Hussars was, however, merely a steppingstone to the next goal of Haig's military career: Staff College.

After his first attempt to enter the college failed due to the discovery that he was color-blind, he was finally accepted in 1896. Haig worked hardest at practical subjects, being content to just get by in courses that were theoretical in

A Hussar cavalryman sits tall in the saddle. Haig joined the elite Seventh Hussars cavalry regiment in 1885.

An Ordinary Soldier

Military history is replete with stories of daring exploits and great victories achieved by military geniuses. During World War I, General Douglas Haig commanded the greatest British army ever assembled to that time. And yet he was by no stretch of the imagination a genius. Indeed, in Winston Churchill's book *Great Contemporaries*, Haig appears as an ordinary man placed in extraordinary circumstances:

> Haig's mind . . . was thoroughly orthodox and conventional. He does not appear to have had any original ideas; no one can discern a spark of that mysterious, visionary, often sinister genius which has enabled the great captains of history to dominate the material factors, save slaughter, and confront their foes with the triumph of novel apparitions. He was, we are told, quite friendly to the tanks, but the maneuver of making them would never have occurred to him. He appeared at all times quite unconscious of any theater but the Western Front. There were the Germans in their trenches. Here he stood at the head of an army corps, then of an army, and finally of a group of mighty armies. Hurl them on and keep slogging at it in the best possible way—that was war. It was undoubtedly one way of making war, and in the end there was certainly overwhelming victory.

nature. Again, close friendships eluded him. But after nearly two years at the college he had learned a great deal and, as biographer Charteris wrote, "he carried away with him a belief in the 'educated soldier,' which never afterwards faltered."[95] He left the Staff College in 1897, a captain at age thirty-six, with the coveted letters *psc* ("passed Staff College") after his name.

After Staff College, Haig returned to regimental life, seeing action in the Sudan in 1898 and in the Boer War from 1899 to 1902. In 1904, Haig was promoted to major general, and the next year he married Dorothy Vivian. Of their whirlwind courtship (he had proposed to Dorothy just two days after they met, and they were married less than a month later) Haig commented, "Why not? I have often made up my mind on more important problems than that of my own marriage in much less time."[96]

Assigned to the War Office from 1906 to 1909, Haig helped create the Imperial General Staff and organize the British Expeditionary Force. In 1912 Haig took command at Aldershot, Britain's premier military training installation. His task there was to shape the British Expeditionary Force into an efficient fighting machine for the European war that, by then, seemed inevitable. And he would have just two short years to do it.

World at War

"This war," Haig wrote on August 4, 1914, the day Britain declared war on Germany, "will last many months, possibly years, so I venture to hope that our only bolt . . . may not suddenly be shot on a project of which success seems to be quite doubtful—I mean the checking of the German advance into France."[97] Even at this early stage, Haig knew that the war would not be over quickly and that his country shouldn't jump into the hostilities too soon. But Britain could not idly stand by while Belgium's neutrality was being trampled by German troops who were pushing their way through Belgium toward France. On August 16, General Douglas Haig, commander of the I Corps of the British Expeditionary Force, landed in France.

The BEF consisted of about one hundred thousand men, including Haig's I Corps, the II Corps commanded by General Horace Smith-Dorrien, and a cavalry division. After fighting off the Germans at Landrecies, for thirteen days Haig supervised his I Corps in an orderly retreat that allowed his men time to recover and prepare to fight again. They would soon get their chance at the ancient town of Ypres.

First Battle of Ypres

As the two sides battled on, each tried to gain an advantage by cutting around the enemy's northern side. This flanking maneuver became known as the "race to the sea," although reaching the coast was never really the objective. The British Expeditionary Force also headed north, to the region of Flanders and the Belgian town of Ypres. If the Germans captured the town they would gain control of the roads leading to the important ports on the English Channel.

On October 21, 1914, Haig's forces engaged the Germans, which he found to be "in considerably greater strength than had originally been anticipated."[98] By efficient management of the defensive line, reinforcing weak areas, and shifting fresh troops to relieve the battle-weary, Haig held off the German advance. But by the end of October the Germans renewed their assault, this time attacking the village of Gheluvelt several miles east of Ypres. As Haig watched his wounded and disheartened troops slowly retreating down the road back to Ypres he mounted his horse, determined to assess the situation for himself. The British *Official History of the War*, tells of Haig "moving up the road at a slow trot with part of his staff behind him as at an inspection, doing much to restore confidence."[99]

The British Expeditionary Force held the line, but at a cost of some 58,000 casualties. A swift German victory had been prevented; in its place would be four years of mud and blood in a stalemate known as trench warfare.

Commander in Chief

On the day after Christmas in 1914, Douglas Haig, now a full general, received a present. The British Expeditionary Force was divided into two armies, and Haig commanded the First Army. He would hold this position throughout 1915 as his army engaged in several ineffectual battles. In March an offensive at Neuve Chapelle resulted in the loss of more than 12,000 men, and in September the Battle of Loos cost another 50,000 British casualties. The first was a limited success, the latter a costly failure.

In December 1915 Haig succeeded Sir John French as commander in chief of the British Expeditionary Force. French had made several miscalculations in strategy that contributed to his removal from command. But intrigue also played a part in Haig's promotion. The ambitious Haig had been sending secret messages to King George V detailing Sir John's shortcomings as a military commander.

As the new year of 1916 began, Haig looked forward to beginning his new command. He had often remarked, "We cannot hope to win until we have defeated the German Army."[100] On July 1, 1916, Haig launched the battle that he felt could do just that—the Battle of the Somme.

A Deadly Day

After nearly two years of war, Britain had lost most of its experienced troops. For his assault on the Somme, Douglas Haig knew that he would have to rely on young and inexperienced soldiers. "I have not got an Army in France, really," he wrote, "but a collection of divisions untrained for the Field."[101] Complicated maneuvers would be beyond these troops; only a direct frontal assault would have a chance of succeeding.

The operation began with a weeklong artillery barrage designed to destroy the German defenses. At 7:30 on the morning of July 1, 1916, British officers blew whistles to signal the start of the assault. One hundred fifty thousand British soldiers scrambled out of the trenches, advancing slowly across no man's land in orderly ranks. Suddenly the sound of machine guns rattled from the German trenches and British soldiers began falling as line upon line were

British troops prepare for battle in Somme, France. On the first day of the Battle of the Somme, 60,000 British soldiers were killed.

cut down by the withering fire. Deep in underground shelters, many German soldiers had survived the initial bombardment and were now paying back the British with deadly efficiency.

The British Army lost nearly 60,000 soldiers that day, the most devastating one-day loss in British military history. At first unaware of the magnitude of the casualties, Haig remained optimistic. But as the weeks wore on and the casualties increased, Haig's confidence began to falter: "I think we have a good chance of success," he wrote to his wife on July 13. "If we don't succeed this time, we'll do so the next! The enemy is, I think, feeling the strain of continuous fighting, and is not fighting so well."[102]

Always interested in new military technology, on September 15, Haig introduced a new weapon to the battle: the tank. Developed in secrecy, tanks were designed to roll across trenches and crush barbed wire. Although Haig had requested 150 of these new machines, fewer than fifty were delivered. In a less than spectacular debut, many tanks broke down or were stranded by the cratered terrain. Inexperienced drivers and infantry troops who had never even seen a tank before added to the confusion. Haig was blamed for revealing Britain's secret weapon before it was ready. War Secretary David Lloyd George wrote that "the great secret was sold for the battered ruin of a little hamlet on the Somme, which was not worth capturing."[103] It would not be the last time the two men would cross paths.

As casualties mounted, so did criticism of Douglas Haig's leadership. A note circulated within the government asked, "Are we to continue until we have killed *all* our young men?"[104] With another winter approaching, however, the Battle of the Somme ended on November 18, 1916. The breakthrough that Haig envisioned had eluded him. Instead, the German line had been pushed back a mere six miles. And for each mile gained, 100,000 Allied soldiers gave their lives.

Passchendaele

Despite the criticism, on January 1, 1917, Douglas Haig received a promotion to field marshal, the highest rank in the British army. Just three weeks before, David Lloyd George had become British prime minister. Their mutual dislike was readily evident. Lloyd George considered Haig an inept general, and was confounded by his inability to communicate clearly. Haig, Lloyd George sarcastically commented, was "Brilliant to the tops of his army boots."[105] For his part, Haig wrote his wife that, "I have no great opinion of L. G. as a man or a leader."[106]

The year 1917 also saw the Russians leave the war, the Americans enter it, and the French army plunge into mutiny. After three years of war and millions of casualties, both the French and German armies were exhausted and running out of reserve forces. But Haig was confident that his British Expeditionary Force could break through the German lines. And he decided to return to Ypres to do it.

The Germans held a strategic ridge near the little town of Passchendaele, several miles northeast of Ypres. If Haig could capture the ridge he had a good chance of gaining ground all the way to the coast. But he would be fighting not only Germans, but Prime Minister Lloyd George as well. The casualties of the Somme still fresh in his mind, Lloyd George was reluctant to approve Haig's plan. At the last moment, however, the prime minister relented; Haig would have his chance.

German troops test captured British tanks (already redecorated with German insignia). Haig was blamed for sending the tanks into battle before they were ready.

As usual, an artillery bombardment preceded the initial attack. But this time the barrage destroyed the region's drainage system, assuring that any rain would turn the fields of Flanders into a morass of thick, oozing mud. On July 31, 1917, the British forces moved out, advancing about two

A Loyal Soldier

As World War I dragged on and casualties increased at a horrifying pace, many in the British government put the blame squarely on their commander in chief, General Douglas Haig. Winston Churchill was first lord of the Admiralty during World War I, and would later become Britain's prime minister and a leading figure in World War II. In his book *Great Contemporaries*, Churchill describes a Douglas Haig loyal to his government despite bitter criticism:

> A selfless, dispassionate, detached equanimity ruled his spirit, not only at moments of acute crisis but month after month and year after year. Inflexible, rigorously pedantic in his assertion of the professional point of view, he nevertheless at all times treated the Civil Power with respect and loyalty. Even when he knew that his recall was debated among the War Cabinet, he neither sought to marshal the powerful political forces which would have come to his aid, nor failed at any time in faithfulness to the Ministers under whom he was serving. Even in the sharpest disagreement he never threatened resignation when he was strong and they were weak. Amid patent ill-success he never in his own technical sphere deferred to their wishes, however strongly those wishes were supported by argument, by public opinion—such as it was—or by the terribly unfolding facts. Right or wrong, victorious or stultified, he remained, within the limits he had marked out for himself, cool and undaunted, ready to meet all emergencies and to accept death or obscurity should either come his way.

late November the battle was over, Haig's breakthrough denied once more. The price: a quarter of a million British lives.

Germany's End Game

Germany's final bid to win the war came on March 21, 1918, with a massive assault against the southern section of the British front. In less than a week German troops had pushed the British line back some twenty-five miles—the first movement in the battlefront since 1914.

Eventually, troops' fatigue and difficulty in getting supplies to the front stopped the initial German drive. But Haig's men were also exhausted, and their ranks were thinning. Knowing that the Germans would try again, Haig asked General Ferdinand Foch, the "generalissimo," or overall commander of the Western Front, for French reinforcements. But Foch declined, preferring to save his soldiers for a counteroffensive.

The second German advance began on April 9 against the British First and Second Armies. Once more Haig appealed to Foch for help, but the generalissimo "replied that the British forces must hold on where they stood and that he could not guarantee any more reinforcements."[107] Haig now had nothing left but words and the will to win. Although he had always been inarticulate in speech, his written order of the day eloquently inspired his weary soldiers: "Many amongst us now are tired. To those I would say that victory will belong to the side which holds out longest. . . . There is no other course open to us but to fight it out! Every

miles the first day. Then the rains came, and continued for weeks. The advance slowed to a crawl as troops and supplies struggled to navigate the ever-present mud. In the end the town of Passchendaele was taken, but little else was accomplished. By position must be held to the last man: there must be no retirement. With our backs to the wall, and believing in the justice of our cause, each one of us must fight on to the end. The safety of our homes and the freedom of mankind alike depend on the conduct of each one of us at this critical moment."[108]

So fight on to the end they did, and the German advance was halted. For the next few months Haig worked to strengthen his exhausted army. And then it was his turn to attack. Through one hundred days and nine battles, the Allies beat back the Germans on the Western Front. Haig urged his commanders on, telling them that "Risks which a month ago would have been criminal to incur, ought now to be incurred as a duty."[109] With the armistice of November 11, 1918, the war ended. A grateful generalissimo Ferdinand Foch said, "Never at any time in history has the British Army achieved greater results than in this unbroken offensive. . . . The victory was indeed complete."[110]

After the War

"Early in 1919 Lord Haig walked ashore at Dover after the total defeat of Germany and disappeared into private life."[111] Thus did Winston Churchill succinctly characterize the later life of Douglas Haig. While many other World War I leaders continued in the military and helped shape the postwar world, Haig seemed excluded from this honor and responsibility. Perhaps to blame was the personal hostility Prime Minister Lloyd George felt toward Haig, which lasted long after the military hostilities had ceased.

But Douglas Haig was far from idle. He founded the British Legion, an organization dedicated to the welfare of British veterans.

It is likely that Haig was excluded from postwar world planning due to the lingering hostility British Prime Minister Lloyd George (pictured) felt toward him.

In October 1919 he was granted the title of earl and eventually received, as a symbol of appreciation from the British people, his ancestral home of Bemersyde. Haig continued his work on behalf of veterans until his death on January 29, 1928, at the age of sixty-seven.

Haig has been harshly criticized for the massive casualties the British Army sustained under his command. Yet he never engaged in recriminations, never wrote a book justifying his military decisions. For Douglas Haig remained content in the knowledge that he had served his country to the best of his ability. And for the gentleman soldier, that knowledge was enough.

Chapter 6

Ferdinand Foch: The Will to Win

The town of Metz in northeastern France is a place of ancient heritage. It has been destroyed several times in its long history, by the Vandals in 406 and the Huns in 452. In 1870 Metz was once more under assault as the German army laid siege to the city at the beginning of the Franco-Prussian War.

Among those touched by that war were students at the Collège de St. Clément in Metz. For the first time they saw the consequences of war, and many were moved to enlist in the French army. The war made an especially lasting impression on one student, who would later write,

> During the afternoon the inhabitants of the invaded and threatened districts flocked towards the town, giving us our first vision of the consequences of defeat, with its sorrowful exodus of families driven from their homes and marching wearily into the unknown: old men, women, and children, carry-

ing off some few belongings, cattle or furniture, despair in their hearts and misery staring them in the face.[112]

The author, eighteen-year-old Ferdinand Foch, joined the service in an outpouring of patriotic fervor. It was his first small step to what, in another day and another war, would become a great military career. For Ferdinand Foch would become supreme commander, the "generalissimo," of World War I, coordinating the armies of the Allied countries into a powerful fighting machine that would prove victorious over the mighty German army.

Early Life

Nestled in the foothills of the Pyrenees Mountains in southwestern France lies Tarbes, a town with a history dating back to Roman times and where, on October 2, 1851, Ferdinand Foch was born. His family had lived in the picturesque region for generations, making their living in the wool trades. Ferdinand's parents were devout Catholics, and their religious influence had a deep impact on their children. Ferdinand remained devoted to the faith throughout his life; his younger brother Germain would eventually enter the priesthood. But religion was not the only influence on young Ferdinand. His maternal grandfather had fought under Napoléon Bonaparte, and his stories of the glorious days of France's First Empire had an impact as well.

Because his father's civil service job required the family to relocate frequently, Ferdinand attended religious schools in various towns throughout southern France. Showing an early aptitude for mathematics, he soon set his sights on attending the École Polytechnique in Paris, a technical college that led some students into military careers in artillery and engineering. In the fall of 1869 he entered the Collège de St. Clément in Metz, a preparatory school for the École Polytechnique. But his tenure at St. Clément would be interrupted by hostilities between two old rivals: France and Germany.

Eighteen-year-old Ferdinand Foch was at home on summer vacation from St. Clément when France declared war against Germany on July 19, 1870, beginning the Franco-Prussian War. Ferdinand enlisted in the Fourth Infantry Regiment and was sent to Chalon-sur-Saône for training. But this

Ferdinand Foch was the supreme commander of the Allied forces during World War I.

early tour of duty would be short-lived. France surrendered on January 21, 1871, and Ferdinand was mustered out of the service two months later without having seen even a moment of action. He soon returned to St. Clément to resume his studies. But this time the atmosphere was different, for the town of Metz was now under German occupation. "At St. Clément's we had to share quarters with German troops en route through Metz and also with a battalion . . . that was permanently garrisoned in the college buildings. . . . [M]any incidents inevitably resulted, for the Germans were quite determined to make us feel the weight of their victory. By violence and brutality . . . they showed us that they considered it as giving them the right to do whatever they pleased."[113] The memories of Metz would remain with Ferdinand throughout his life.

Military Education

After passing rigorous entrance examinations, Ferdinand Foch was admitted to the École Polytechnique in November 1871. His family had hopes that he would choose one of the civilian vocations for which the Polytechnique prepared its students. Foch, however, had other ideas. "The disastrous war from which we had just emerged . . . imposed upon all of us, and especially upon the youth of the nation, the sacred task of building up our country, now dismembered and constantly menaced with complete destruction. Accordingly, without hesitation I joined those students who were volunteering for the artillery, known by the sobriquet of 'the little hats.'"[114] After fifteen months at the Polytechnique he entered the École d'Application d'Artillerie, or artillery school.

Little information survives concerning Foch's military education. But his later writings reveal the beginnings of a concept that would influence his military career: "I pursued with single purpose my military ambition. I strove to apply the conclusions of an essay which had been given us to work upon at St. Clément, at the very moment when the country was being invaded by those Germans whom I meant one day to drive out: 'Youth must train its gifts.'

The Franco-Prussian War

World War I was not the first conflict between the great European powers of France and Germany. After suffering a military defeat at the hands of France in 1806, Prussia, the predominant state of the German Empire, began to rebuild its army. Prussia's swift defeat of Austria in 1866 appeared to lay the groundwork for a new campaign against France.

A scheme to install a Prussian prince on the throne of Spain in 1868 caused France to fear being encircled by hostile German territories. Inflamed by public opinion, France declared war on Prussia on July 19, 1870. But with an army only half the size of Prussia's, France was no match for her enemy's efficient military machine. The French concentrated their forces around the cities of Sedan and Metz but soon found themselves surrounded. The war seemed to be over almost before it began.

On September 1, 1870, the French army at Sedan surrendered more than 100,000 troops to the Prussians. Less than two months later Metz fell. The Prussian army then turned its attention to Paris, besieging the city until it, too, capitulated. On January 28, 1871, an armistice was signed, ending the Franco-Prussian War.

The humiliating defeat cost France an indemnity of five billion gold francs and most of the provinces of Alsace and Lorraine. But it would cost the world even more, as a French desire for revenge, and Germany's fear of that revenge, set the stage for an even more devastating conflict that would be known as World War I.

There is the whole secret. Our gifts must be bent towards the one essential goal, the act of willing."[115]

On October 1, 1873, the day before his twenty-second birthday, Ferdinand Foch graduated from the École d'Application, receiving his commission as a second lieutenant in the artillery. The next year he began his military career in earnest, joining the Twenty-fourth Artillery Regiment in his hometown of Tarbes.

Teaching the Troops

Over the next decade Foch served in several regimental and staff assignments in both the artillery and the cavalry, attaining the rank of captain in 1878. Stationed for a time in Brittany in the northwest of France, Foch fell in love with the region known for its history and the devout character of its people. He also fell in love with a young lady named Julie Bienvenue, whom he married in 1883. Brittany would become Foch's home and his refuge for the remainder of his life.

In 1885 Foch enrolled as a student at the École Supérieur de Guerre, or War College, where he was taught by a faculty of excellent instructors. He would return to the college as an instructor in 1895, and again in 1908, when he was personally appointed commandant of the school by French premier Georges Clemenceau. It would not be the last time that the two men's paths would cross.

At the École Polytechnique, Foch volunteered for artillery school and trained in a unit like this one. After graduating, he was commissioned as a second lieutenant in artillery.

After a year as an assistant instructor of tactics, Foch advanced to chief instructor in 1896, a post he would hold for the next five years. He soon gained a reputation as an important military thinker and an excellent lecturer. Foch wrote two books setting forth the essence of his lectures at the college: *The Principles of War* (1903) and *On the Conduct of War* (1904). The *attaque à outrance* or "attack to the utmost" was a key point in Foch's teachings. "Offensive action, whether adopted immediately or following a defensive one, alone can produce results, and consequently must always be adopted, at any rate in the long run."[116] But true to his earlier education, Foch also placed great emphasis on the will to win. "A battle won is a battle in which one cannot admit that one is beaten. . . . The will to conquer is the first condition for victory, and consequently the first duty of every soldier."[117]

A Different Kind of War

Germany's blueprint for war was known as the Schlieffen Plan. It called for a massive assault through Belgium with a limited southern advance from the former French provinces of Alsace and Lorraine, occupied by Germany since the Franco-Prussian War. In August 1914 sixty-three-year-old Ferdinand Foch, now a brigadier general, was in command of the Twentieth Army Corps at Nancy, an industrial city on the frontier between France and Germany. On the alert for signs of enemy action, Foch's troops were involved in only minor skir-

Foch the Educator

Although at the time Ferdinand Foch had no experience in actual combat, his lectures at the École de Guerre were nonetheless popular with his students. In addition to his bold theories concerning offensive strategy, Foch also had a persuasive style of lecturing. One of his contemporaries wrote of Foch in the classroom, as quoted here from James Marshall-Cornwall's book, *Foch as Military Commander:*

> Lieutenant-Colonel Foch did not disappoint [his students]. Slim, good-looking, with an air of refinement . . . one was at once struck by his look of energy, calmness, and rectitude. His forehead was broad, his nose proud and straight, his gray-blue eyes looked one straight in the face. He spoke without gesture, with authority and conviction. His voice was deep, gruff and a little monotonous. He used long sentences to take in all the detours of a rigorous reasoning. He pushed on the discussion, always appealing to logic, and often even having recourse to mathematical terms. Sometimes he was difficult to follow, for there was such a wealth of ideas in his lectures, but he always held the attention of his hearers by the clear-sightedness of his views and his tone of sincerity. By common consent of his students, Colonel Foch was regarded as the most profound and the most original of all the teachers of the Staff College. . . . From their first introduction to him they were only too willing to follow his lessons and share his enthusiasm.

mishes. Then on August 14, 1914, the French Second Army, of which Foch's corps was a part, began an assault on German troops at Morhange in Lorraine. At first little resistance was encountered, but before long, enemy artillery was inflicting devastating losses on the French forces.

In combat the diminutive five-foot-six-inch-tall Foch proved to be a no-nonsense commander. A contemporary writer commented, "The French leader has the reputation for being very reserved and quite distant in his manner. His orders are given very briefly and, when busy with war and its works, he is a man of very few words. He hardly makes addresses to the soldiers; in fact, they would like to have him exhort them more than he does."[118]

It soon became clear to Foch that fighting a modern war would be very different from the theories he had taught at the War College. And the tragedy inherent in such a war would become personal for Foch when his only son, Germain, and his son-in-law were killed in action on the same day, August 22, 1914. Due to the difficulties of communicating on the battlefield, it would take three weeks for the sorrowful news to reach Foch.

Battle of the Marne

Although his attacks had been repulsed by the German army, Foch's leadership skills made a favorable impression on General Joseph Joffre, the French commander in chief. In late August, Joffre had a new assignment for Foch. French units had pulled back as the Germans advanced, creating a gap between the French Fourth and Fifth Armies. Foch, as commander of the newly formed Ninth Army, was to use his troops to fill that gap. He commented on the dangerous situation: "In consequence of this gap, the German Third Army had encountered no opposition during its march forward, and it was beginning seriously to outflank our Fourth Army's left. This was the danger that my detachment was called upon to guard against."[119]

Only a week after taking command, Foch led his army in a defensive battle along a twenty-mile front. On September 8, 1914, Foch's troops halted the German advance at the Battle of the Marne, but they were still under tremendous pressure to hold the line against a superior enemy. Legend has it that at this critical time, Foch sent a bold message to headquarters: "I am hard pressed on my right; my center is giving way; situation excellent; I am attacking."[120] As Lieutenant Colonel Maxime Weygand, Foch's chief of staff recalled, "these words were never uttered, but the truth is equally fine; they symbolize the energy, resolution and confidence which he displayed throughout the battle."[121] Foch's troops held the line and the German advance was halted.

On October 4, 1914, General Joffre appointed Foch his deputy and placed him in command of the Northern Army Group. Foch's designation as Joffre's assistant made him the second most powerful officer in the French army. It would also nearly destroy his career.

In the Trenches

With the year 1915 came a change in the conduct of the war as both sides settled into trench warfare. Foch gradually realized that the *attaque à outrance* would not win this war. "This meeting of two great armies after forty years of peace was bringing astonishing changes in the practice of war. As time went on our tactics became adapted to the new conditions."[122]

From his headquarters at Doullens, Foch was to coordinate the operations of French, British, and Belgian troops. Dealing with soldiers from other Allied nations gave Foch valuable experience for his future career. "He never utters a complaint or reproach," wrote Colonel Weygand, "to those with whom he is associated in the struggle. . . . Much good grace, tact and warmth temper his strength. Thus he manages to inspire decisions, and to animate their execution with his own ardor."[123]

But even Foch's ardor, his will to win, wasn't always enough to insure victory on the battlefield. Throughout 1915 and 1916, French and British troops fought bloody battles for virtually no gain in territory. At Artois, Foch's offensive began promisingly with the capture of Vimy Ridge. But the drive ultimately stalled, costing the French some 100,000 casualties. The Battle of the Somme was launched on July 1, 1916, to relieve pressure on the

French soldiers capture German machine guns during the Battle of the Marne. Foch's men halted the German advance and held the line under tremendous pressure.

French casualties numbered more than 200,000 in the Battle of the Somme, a five-month battle that ended in a stalemate.

fortress city of Verdun and break through the German lines. Foch, in charge of the British and French forces involved in the assault, had fewer units to draw from than he had planned. After five months the battle ended in a stalemate, with French casualties numbering more than 200,000.

Out of Favor

The bloody Battle of the Somme created sweeping changes in the French army. Seeking a scapegoat for the losses of the Somme, General Joseph Joffre relieved Foch as head of the Northern Armies Group. Foch accepted his fate calmly and with dignity, never uttering a word of recrimination against his commander in chief. But removing Foch did not save Joffre's career: in what was officially described as a promotion, Joffre was moved to another assignment.

Throughout 1917 Foch carried out several minor consulting assignments, including a trip to Italy in April 1917 to coordinate defensive strategies at the Italian front. He would return to Italy in October after Austrian and German troops began a massive offensive at Caporetto. Foch quickly arranged to bring French and

British troops to the Italian front, displaying once more his skill at coordinating the forces of various countries.

The Battle of Caporetto confirmed the need for a "unified command" to better coordinate the Allied armies. At a conference at Rapallo, Italy, in November 1917, officials of the French, British, and Italian governments created the Supreme War Council. Foch became France's military representative on the council. Then on November 16 a political event occurred that would have a profound effect on Foch's military career. Georges Clemenceau, who had fallen out of favor with the government, once again became France's premier. Clemenceau realized that a truly unified command would require an overall leader, or "generalissimo," to efficiently direct the Allied forces. He envisioned Foch as his generalissimo, but British prime minister David Lloyd George opposed the idea of an overall commander. Events in early 1918, however, would work to change his mind.

The Germans Attack

"We must prepare ourselves for a very serious offensive on the part of the Germans any moment after the commencement of this year,"[124] wrote Ferdinand Foch to the Supreme War Council in a report on January 1, 1918. He went on to describe how the Allies should counter this offensive. "We will meet this attack by defensive dispositions which at this moment are being carried out on the British and French fronts. . . . But we ought also . . . to seize every opportunity to impose [our] will upon the adversary. This can only be done through assuming the offensive the moment it is possible; for by no other means can victory be attained."[125]

On the morning of March 21, 1918, the thunderous pounding of thousands of artillery pieces heralded the German assault. Five days later, with German troops threatening to divide the Allied armies, Foch was appointed "coordinator" of the French and British forces on the Western Front. But a

British soldiers man artillery located on the Western Front.

coordinator was not a commander, and Foch's authority was limited. While he could provide overall strategic direction to the armies, battlefield control remained with the British and French commanders in chief. Furthermore, the commanders could appeal Foch's decisions to their respective heads of government.

Generalissimo

Foch immediately went to work, visiting the headquarters of the Allied armies. He instilled in his commanders the will to keep fighting and organized the mobilization of reserve troops to strengthen the weakest parts of the Allied lines. On April 14, 1918, the Supreme War Council named Foch commander in chief of the Allied armies—the generalissimo that Clemenceau had wanted. Finally, unified command of the Allied forces was a reality.

For the next several months the Germans continued to pound the Allied lines with a series of surprise attacks. Foch continued the defensive plan he had outlined on January 1, shuttling his reserves to meet each new assault. By July the German offensive was slowly grinding to a halt. The German soldiers were exhausted and unable to exploit their breakthroughs because of delays in receiving supplies and replacement troops. Foch saw that the time was right to begin the offensive phase of his plan. "After four months on the defensive, imposed upon us by the enemy's numerical superiority, a victorious counteroffensive had once more placed in our hands

the initiative of operations and the power to direct the progress of events in this long, vast war."[126]

Foch launched the Allied counteroffensive on July 18, 1918. French forces along with newly arrived American troops hit the enemy in a series of limited offensives designed not to create a decisive breakthrough, but to apply constant pressure on the German lines. On August 8 an Allied offensive from the town of Amiens drove the Germans back with the help of some 435 British tanks. It was a day that the German commander, General Erich Ludendorff, called the "black day of the German Army,"[127] for he knew that Germany could no longer win the war. While Ludendorff was contemplating his inevitable defeat, just two days earlier Foch had been rewarded with a promotion to marshal of France for his leadership as generalissimo.

Armistice

Through the months of September and October 1918 the German army was everywhere in retreat. On October 24 Foch met with Clemenceau to discuss the military terms of an armistice with Germany. Foch had already drawn up a list of conditions that Germany would have to accept in return for a cease-fire. These included the evacuation of German troops from the territories they had invaded (including Alsace and Lorraine); the surrender of thousands of artillery pieces, machine guns, and other war material; and the immediate withdrawal of German forces to the east side of the

On November 8, 1918, the armistice agreement ending World War I was signed in this railroad car.

Rhine River. When asked if he thought it would be better to continue the war rather than seek an armistice, Foch replied, "I am not waging war for the sake of waging war. If I obtain through the Armistice the conditions that we wish to impose on Germany, I am satisfied. Once this object is obtained, nobody has the right to shed one drop more of blood."[128]

Marshal Foch had, in fact, made plans for an Allied offensive to take place on November 15, 1918. But it would not be necessary. Germany knew it was defeated and now had to find a way to end the war as favorably as possible.

"My Work Is Finished"

At 7 A.M. on November 8, 1918, a train squealed to a halt on a track hidden in the Compiègne Forest near the town of Rethondes, France. The train carried a German delegation seeking an end to World War I. Some one hundred yards away, on a siding originally built for rail-mounted artillery, sat a similar train. It contained only three cars, a dining car, a parlor car, and a sleeping car. But in this train peace would be made.

A few minutes after 9 A.M. the German group entered the dining car of the second train, where the Allied delegation, headed by Marshal Ferdinand Foch, waited. After brief, formal introductions everyone sat down, the Germans facing the others across the table. In a voice filled with contempt, Foch tersely addressed his interpreter: "Ask these gentlemen what they want."[129] After the Germans announced their desire for a cease-fire, the terms of the armistice were read. After relaying the terms to their government and haggling for concessions, the German delegation finally signed the armistice agreement three days later. When Foch reported the signing to Clemenceau, the prime minister congratulated his generalissimo. Foch then replied, "My work is finished; your work begins."[130] At 11 A.M. on November 11, 1918, the eleventh hour of the eleventh day of the eleventh month, the guns fell silent, signifying the end of World War I.

If Ferdinand Foch's work was finished, the honors bestowed upon him were not. But despite numerous accolades, the war's end brought a decline in Foch's influence. For although the military had defeated Germany, politicians would now decide Germany's fate.

In January 1919, peace talks convened in Paris. Foch had hopes that Germany would be severely punished to once and for all prevent further aggression. As the conference wore on, he felt that Clemenceau, negotiating for France, was not harsh enough in his dealings with the defeated nation. But Foch never considered entering politics, where he might have been able to advance his ideas for a postwar world.

After the war, Foch received numerous honors. In 1919 he became a member of the prestigious Académie Française. Great Britain honored Foch's wartime leadership by making him a Field Marshal. It was the first time a Frenchman had received such an honor since Jean-Louis, Earl Ligonier, was appointed in 1757. In 1921 Foch garnered further accolades during a triumphant tour of the United States.

On March 20, 1929, Marshal Ferdinand Foch died in Paris. He was, fittingly, buried near the tomb of Napoléon, the French emperor whose daring exploits had inspired him as a child in Tarbes. In life Ferdinand Foch had embodied the will to win; in death he would be remembered as the man who won the war and saved France.

☆ Chapter 7 ☆

Woodrow Wilson: Crusader for Peace

For three weeks in the autumn of 1919 a special seven-car train had been rolling across America, making stops in such places as St. Louis, Kansas City, San Francisco, and other cities of the Midwestern and Western states. As the rugged American landscape rushed past the windows, President Woodrow Wilson sat in the last car, writing yet another speech for the next stop on the grueling twenty-two-day journey. For Wilson the trip was nothing less than a crusade, a sacred mission to convince the American people that the United States must ratify the Treaty of Versailles.

The treaty that ended World War I embodied Wilson's greatest dream: the League of Nations, an organization of countries bound together to preserve peace and prevent another devastating global conflict. For three years Wilson had struggled to keep the United States out of the war. When circumstances finally forced America to enter the war, he acted quickly and decisively to mobilize the military and industrial might of the nation. But Woodrow Wilson never abandoned his commitment to world peace, and worked tirelessly to create a league dedicated to a future without recriminations or territorial disputes.

The U.S. Senate, however, balked at American participation in the League of Nations, so Wilson decided to take his plan to the people. The president knew all too well what the arduous trip could cost him. "Even though in my condition," he confided to an aide, "it might mean the giving up of my life, I will gladly make the sacrifice to save the Treaty."[131]

At age sixty-two, in fragile health and suffering from blinding headaches, Woodrow Wilson was determined to fight to the end for his beloved League of Nations. But as the special train pulled into Pueblo, Colorado, on the afternoon of September 25, 1919, the end was closer than even Wilson himself could know.

Preacher's Son

Thomas Woodrow Wilson was born in the small town of Staunton, Virginia, on December 28, 1856. His father, Joseph Ruggles Wilson, was a Presbyterian minister, a tall, articulate preacher who was proud of his Scotch-Irish ancestry. Janet "Jessie" Woodrow Wilson, Thomas's mother, could trace her background to Scotland as well, where her ancestors included several distinguished clergymen. A stately, white-columned parsonage in Staunton was the Wilson home until Joseph accepted a new calling in Augusta, Georgia, and moved his family there in 1857.

Thomas, the third of four children, inherited his parents' Scottish seriousness and devotion to causes they held dear. Joseph was especially influential on Thomas, teaching his son the importance of faith and encouraging him to develop precision in the spoken and written word. Thomas also inherited his father's sense of humor, and in his years of public service often enjoyed telling humorous stories and limericks.

A Southern Education

Growing up in the South during and after the Civil War, Thomas Woodrow Wilson's early education was irregular at best. Modern historians believe Thomas suffered from dyslexia, because he was nine years old before he learned the alphabet and nearly twelve before he could read well. He was taught at home until age nine, when he began his formal education at a private school in Augusta run by a former Confederate officer. When in 1870 his father moved the family once more, this time to Columbia, South Carolina, Thomas attended a private school across the street from his house.

President Woodrow Wilson's greatest dream was the establishment of a league of nations.

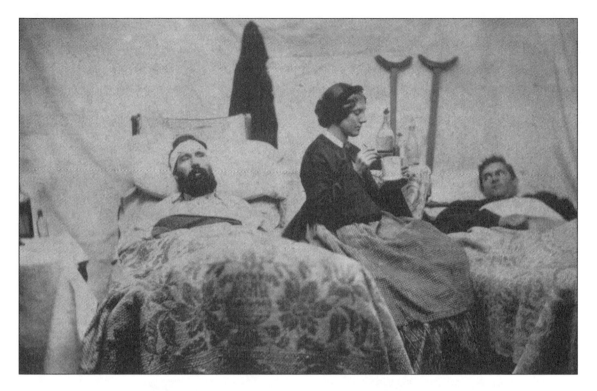

During the Civil War, Wilson saw the tragic effects of war firsthand when his father's church became a makeshift hospital.

Thomas studied mathematics and science, some Latin, and American history. Although his infirmities later in life have led some to conclude that Thomas was a sickly child, he was, in fact a normal boy who played baseball and went horseback riding. He was highly imaginative, acting out scenes from books he had read or pretending he was an admiral on the high seas. At age fifteen he taught himself shorthand, perhaps a result of his continuing difficulty in writing.

There was one aspect of his education, however, that no school taught but would profoundly affect his life. During the Civil War his father's church had become a makeshift hospital, and young Thomas was able to see firsthand the tragic effects of war. "A boy never gets over his boyhood," he would later write, "and never can change those subtle influences which have become a part of him."[132] As president of the United States, he would do everything in his power to keep his country out of another devastating conflict.

On To Princeton

In 1873 Thomas entered Davidson College in North Carolina. At Davidson he received good grades, played baseball, and joined the Eumenean Society, a debating club. Yet it was the first time Thomas had been away from his family, and homesickness soon took its toll. In the spring of 1874 he left Davidson and returned home, spending the next year reading and engaging his father in long discussions.

By the spring of 1875 Thomas was ready to leave home again. This time he headed for the College of New Jersey at Princeton. A good but not exceptional student, the lanky young Wilson felt at home at Princeton. Although uninterested in science and mathematics courses, he discovered a true passion for politics and history. He read voraciously and joined the Whig Society, a debating club. Later Wilson showed his talent for organization when he created the Liberal Debating Club, founded, as he wrote in the club's constitution, upon "principles of Justice, Morality, and Friendship."[133]

By his junior year Wilson was becoming a popular student on the Princeton campus. As managing editor of the university newspaper *The Princetonian*, he wrote editorials on various aspects of campus life from athletics to spiritual matters. A highlight of his Princeton years was the sale of an essay entitled "Cabinet Government in the United States" to *International Review* magazine. It was his first published article.

Law and Academe

After graduating from Princeton in 1879, Thomas Woodrow Wilson decided on a career in politics. "The profession I chose was politics; the profession I entered was the law.

I entered the one because I thought it would lead to the others. It was once the sure road; and Congress is still full of lawyers."[134]

Wilson entered the law school at the University of Virginia in the fall of 1879. He soon discovered, however, that he had little taste for the intricacies of legal studies. He wrote to a friend, "I wish now to record the confession that I am most terribly bored by the noble study of Law sometimes."[135] Wilson left the university in December 1880 to complete his law studies at home. Although he passed the bar exam and even opened a law office in Atlanta, he knew that practicing law was not for him. He decided instead to pursue a teaching career, receiving a Ph.D. degree from Johns Hopkins University in 1886.

After a time teaching at Bryn Mawr College in Pennsylvania and Wesleyan University in Connecticut, in 1890 Wilson accepted a professorship at his alma mater, Princeton. By this time he had wed Ellen Louise Axson, a happy marriage that would give them three daughters. He had also dropped his first name, Thomas, referring to himself for the rest of his life as Woodrow Wilson.

Political Ambitions

For twelve years Woodrow Wilson was a professor of "jurisprudence and political economy" at Princeton. When the university president left office in 1902, Wilson was unanimously chosen to fill the vacancy. He established himself as a progressive reformer, instituting the "preceptor" system, wherein students worked closely with assistant professors to concentrate on their fields of interest.

Wilson's proposal to eliminate Princeton's exclusive "eating clubs" (similar to fraternities) caused a stir in the university. And when he advocated placing Princeton's independent graduate school under his control, the resulting controversy forced him to resign in 1910.

From his years at Princeton, Woodrow Wilson had become a nationally known figure. In June 1910 he was chosen by the Democratic Party in New Jersey as their candidate for governor. Wilson promised that, if elected, he would resist "the dictation of any person or persons, special interests or organizations."[136] Easily winning the election, Wilson made good on his promise, going so far as to oppose a Senate bid by James Smith Jr., a powerful Democratic Party boss.

Wilson's political career quickly gathered momentum. Talk of Woodrow Wilson for president began to circulate. His campaign speech of May 26, 1912, gives a revealing look into Woodrow Wilson's early ideas for world peace: "I believe that God

As a professor, and later a president, of Princeton University, Wilson became a nationally known figure.

planted in us visions of liberty . . . that we are chosen and prominently chosen to show the way to the nations of the world how they shall walk in the paths of liberty."[137] At the Democratic Party convention in June 1912 he received his party's nomination for president on the forty-sixth ballot.

Victory in the election of 1912 was a virtual certainty for Wilson. The rival Republicans were split when Theodore Roosevelt broke away and formed his own progressive party, nicknamed the "Bull Moose" party. This drew Republican votes away from the current president, William Howard Taft, assuring his defeat. When the votes were tallied on November 5, 1912, Woodrow Wilson had become the twenty-eighth president of the United States.

An Ironic Presidency

"It would be the irony of fate if my administration had to deal chiefly with foreign affairs."[138] This statement expresses Woodrow Wilson's hope that, as president, he could concentrate on making progressive reforms at home. He called his plan the New Freedom, and he put it into effect soon after entering office. He reformed tariff laws, created the Federal Reserve System to oversee the banking industry, and fought for antitrust legislation.

But while President Wilson was carrying out his reforms at home, things were heating up abroad. After revolutionary general Victoriano Huerta seized control of Mexico in February 1913, Wilson refused to recognize what he called "a government of butch-ers."[139] Eventually three countries, Argentina, Brazil, and Chile (dubbed the "ABC" countries), stepped in to mediate the Mexican dispute. In 1916 Wilson would experience further problems south of the border, sending General John J. "Black Jack" Pershing to Mexico to break up a terrorist gang led by the notorious guerrilla Francisco "Pancho" Villa.

War and Neutrality

Wilson's foreign affairs troubles did not end at the Mexican border. On August 4, 1914, German troops stormed through neutral Belgium on their way toward Paris and, so they thought, a swift victory. When Great Britain declared war on Germany the next day, Wilson issued a statement proclaiming America's neutrality in the European conflict. Wilson was deeply distressed by the war, for he wrote, "I feel the burden of the thing almost intolerably from day to day."[140] He was to suffer another, more personal burden just days after the war began.

Ellen Wilson had fallen ill that spring and was diagnosed with chronic nephritis, a serious kidney ailment. As her condition worsened, Wilson held out hope that she would recover. But on August 6, 1914, Ellen died with Woodrow by her bedside, holding her hand to the end. The stricken president could only murmur over and over, "Oh, my God, what am I going to do? What am I going to do?"[141]

What he had to do, of course, was carry on with his presidency. In his grief, Wilson pushed aside his personal life in order to

Ellen Wilson died of a kidney ailment in 1914. Wilson was forced to set aside his grief and address escalating international tensions.

handle the tasks at hand. To a friend he wrote that "the less I analyze my feelings the better. . . . Woodrow Wilson does not matter, but the United States does and all that it may accomplish for its own people and the people of the world outside of it."[142]

That world by the end of 1914 had descended into a bloody war of stagnation. Opposing lines of trenches coursed like open wounds across the French countryside, and shell craters pocked the "no man's land" in between. While generally favoring the Allied cause, Woodrow Wilson repeatedly called for American neutrality. After all, the war had yet to touch the United States, safely located an ocean away from the carnage.

But that was about to change. On May 7, 1915, the British passenger ship *Lusitania* was torpedoed without warning by a German submarine. Among the nearly 1,200 people who perished in the sinking were 128 Americans. Cries of outrage and revenge echoed across America. But Wilson stood by his conviction that the United States remain above those nations that had descended into the madness of war: "The example of America must be a special example. . . . There is such a thing as a man being too proud to fight. There is such a thing as a nation being so right that it does not need to convince others by force that it is right."[143] Wilson sent a protest to the German government and ultimately obtained a pledge that no more passenger ships would be sunk.

One hundred twenty-eight Americans perished when the British passenger ship Lusitania *was torpedoed by a German submarine.*

Woodrow Wilson had resolved a difficult situation while keeping the United States from entering the war. That fact would become the theme of his reelection campaign in 1916: "He Kept Us Out Of War." On the strength of this achievement, Wilson was reelected by a narrow margin in November 1916. By this time a new first lady had joined him in the White House, for on December 18, 1915, Woodrow Wilson married his second wife, Edith Bolling Galt.

War . . . and Peace

Wilson still desperately longed for a way to resolve the European conflict in a peaceful manner. But circumstances finally made America's entry into the war inevitable. Germany announced that on February 1, 1917, unrestricted submarine warfare would resume. The president now had no choice but to break off diplomatic relations with Germany. On April 2, after three American ships had been torpedoed, Wilson asked Congress for a declaration of war. His aim was not conquest but the noble ideal of freedom for all people. On April 6, President Wilson signed the official proclamation of war with Germany.

As the nation spent the following months mobilizing its military forces, Woodrow Wilson continued to search for a plan to end the war. With his close aide Edward House, Wilson worked out a fourteen-point proposal for world peace. On January 8, 1918, Wilson presented his "Fourteen Points" to a joint session of Congress. For Wilson the most important point was Number 14, the establishment of a League of Nations to prevent future wars.

By the fall of 1918 the Allies, with the help of U.S. troops led by General John J. Pershing, had the German army on the run. When the armistice came on November 11, 1918, there was rejoicing throughout the world. But the armistice was merely a temporary halt in the hostilities. A permanent peace treaty would have to be hammered out among the leaders of the belligerent nations. On December 4, 1918, Woodrow Wilson set sail for France with the hope that his League of Nations would finally be born.

Paris

As confident as Wilson was about the merits of the Fourteen Points, during the voyage he expressed a hint of doubt about the peace talks. "What I seem to see—with all my heart I hope I am wrong—is a tragedy of disappointment."[144] But when he arrived in France on December 13, his doubts were, at least temporarily, dispelled. A torn and bleeding land greeted Wilson with accolades and jubilation. During a tour of the great European capitals, people knelt along the railroad tracks as his train passed by, waving flags and shouting Wilson's praises. To the people of Europe, Woodrow

A World Safe for Democracy

April 2, 1917 was rainy, a fittingly somber background for what President Woodrow Wilson was about to do. Crowds jammed the streets outside the Capitol. Inside, in the House chamber, every seat was filled. At a special session of Congress that fateful evening, Wilson would ask for a declaration of war against Germany. The following excerpt from Wilson's War Message—which can be found on the Internet at http://www.lib.byu.edu/~rdh/wwi/1917/wilswarm.html—shows the president's vision for a new world of lasting peace and freedom.

The world must be made safe for democracy. Its peace must be planted on the tested foundations of political liberty. We have no selfish ends to serve. We desire no conquest, no dominion. We seek no indemnities for ourselves, no material compensation for the sacrifices we shall freely make. We are but one of the champions of the rights of mankind. We shall be satisfied when those rights have been made as secure as the faith and the freedom of nations can make them.

When Wilson finished his speech, thundering applause and wild cheering filled the House chamber. But as Gene Smith relates in his book, *When the Cheering Stopped*, Woodrow Wilson knew what he had just done. "My message today," Wilson later remarked, "was a message of death for our young men. How strange it seems to applaud that."

Wilson was a savior. But the leaders of the Allied nations were not as enamored with the American president.

Representatives of twenty-seven countries (Germany, as the vanquished nation, would not attend until April, when presented with the final treaty) sat at a long, polished table when the Paris Peace Conference began on January 18, 1919. Only four men, however, would actually lead the peace talks. "The Big Four" were Wilson, British prime minister David Lloyd George, French premier Georges Clemenceau, and Italy's Vittorio Orlando. Tensions arose almost from the very beginning. Clemenceau, for example, poked fun at Wilson's peace plan, joking that while God had created only ten commandments, Wilson needed fourteen.

The peace conference was a test of wills for the Big Four. While Wilson tried to promote "peace without victory," France's Clemenceau was intent on crippling Germany so it could never wage war again. Lloyd George fought to assure continuation of England's vast empire and her domination of the seas. The leaders argued over national boundaries and German reparations. Wilson often found his idealistic plans butting head-on against the harsh realities of European politics. In addition, the grueling conference was taking a toll on Wilson's health.

Journalist Ray Stannard Baker wrote, "Sometimes . . . I went up to see him in the evening after the meetings of the Four, he looked utterly beaten, worn out, his face quite haggard and one side of it and the eye twitching painfully; but the next morning he would appear refreshed and eager to go on with the fight."[145] Eventually Wilson's fighting spirit would win out. On June 28, 1919, the Treaty of Versailles was signed, officially ending World War I. Although Wil-

French premier Georges Clemenceau (with cane) and Woodrow Wilson emerge from the Paris Peace Conference after signing the Treaty of Versailles.

son had agreed to a harsh punishment of Germany, the treaty authorized the establishment of his beloved League of Nations. His goal in Europe achieved, Woodrow Wilson's next task was to convince his own government to ratify the treaty.

Appeal to Caesar

Wilson's fight for the League of Nations at home would be even tougher than the negotiations in Paris. Isolationists in the United States Senate, led by Republican Henry Cabot Lodge, had serious reservations about the League. They objected to the provision that the nations in the League must come to each other's aid if attacked. This, the Republicans said, could entangle the United States in even more European conflicts. With Lodge as chairman of the Senate Foreign Relations Committee, Wilson knew that approval of the League was unlikely. So he decided to take his plan to the people.

Wilson called his national tour an "appeal to Caesar"—a gathering of grassroots support from the people of America. It was to be a triumphant journey that would champion the importance of America's participation in the League of Nations. But by the time Wilson's train reached Pueblo, Colorado, on September 25, the president's health had declined alarmingly. He couldn't sleep and ate erratically. A pounding headache was his constant companion. When First Lady Edith Wilson begged him to cancel the rest of the trip, Wilson, in a tone of forced encouragement, replied,

"Cheer up! This will soon be over. And when we get back to Washington I promise you I'll take a holiday."[146] But there would be no holiday for the ailing president.

As Wilson mounted the platform in Pueblo to speak to a cheering crowd of ten thousand, he stumbled on a step. He also stumbled over his speech, halting and starting over again as he struggled with his words. Woodrow Wilson, a gifted orator, had never had such trouble before. He finally managed to finish his speech and returned to his train to head for the next stop, Wichita, Kansas. The next morning, however, Wilson's speech was slurred and the left side of his face sagged. Alarmed at Wilson's condition, Dr. Cary Grayson, his personal physician, immediately canceled the trip. Soon the president's special train was heading at full speed back to Washington.

No Compromise

Once back at the White House, Wilson's condition improved slightly. The public was told only that he suffered from a "nervous breakdown" and exhaustion. But on October 2, 1919, Edith Wilson found her husband lying unconscious on the bathroom floor. Woodrow Wilson had suffered a massive stroke, leaving his left side immobile and his vision impaired. Dr. Grayson could only exclaim, "My God, the President is paralyzed!"[147] For weeks Wilson hovered between life and death. It would be several months before he could walk just a few steps, aided by a cane. He grew a beard, perhaps to disguise the paralysis to the left side of his face.

As he lay in bed in the White House, Wilson had just one concern: the fight for the League of Nations. Unfortunately, it was not going well. Senator Lodge had introduced fourteen reservations to the Treaty of Versailles. Without these reservations the treaty would not be ratified, and the United States would not join the League of Nations. Aides recommended that he compromise in order to secure approval of the treaty, and a healthy Wilson might have seen the wisdom of such a move. But the disease that crippled his body had also afflicted his mind. He could be irritable and unreasonable, or so

Wilson's Fourteen Points

On January 8, 1918, Woodrow Wilson addressed a joint session of Congress, offering his program for world peace. His fourteen-point plan is printed here, condensed from the original text of the speech, which can be found on the Internet at Northwestern University's Douglass Archives of American Public Address (http://douglass.speech.nwu.edu/wils_a23.htm). The last point, No. 14, outlines Wilson's concept for the League of Nations. It is interesting to note that Wilson wrote the draft of the Fourteen Points, as he did with all his speeches, in shorthand.

1. Open covenants of peace, openly arrived at.

2. Absolute freedom of navigation upon the seas, outside territorial waters, alike in peace and war.

3. The removal . . . of all economic barriers and the establishment of an equality of trade conditions.

4. Adequate guarantees . . . that national armaments will be reduced to the lowest point consistent with domestic safety.

5. A free, open-minded, and absolutely impartial adjustment of all colonial claims.

6. The evacuation of all Russian territory and . . . opportunity for the independent determination of her own political development.

7. Belgium . . . must be evacuated and restored.

8. All French territory should be freed and the invaded portions restored, and the wrong done to France by Prussia in 1871 in the matter of Alsace-Lorraine . . . should be righted.

9. A readjustment of the frontiers of Italy should be effected.

10. The peoples of Austria-Hungary . . . should be accorded the freest opportunity of autonomous development.

11. Rumania, Serbia, and Montenegro should be evacuated; occupied territories restored.

12. The Turkish portions of the present Ottoman Empire should be assured a secure sovereignty, but the other nationalities . . . now under the Turkish rule should be assured . . . an absolutely unmolested opportunity of autonomous development.

13. An independent Polish state should be erected.

14. A general association of nations must be formed under specific covenants for the purpose of affording mutual guarantees of political independence and territorial integrity to great and small states alike.

overly emotional that he would cry for no apparent reason. His ability to concentrate and make rational decisions was impaired. On the possibility of a compromise, Wilson would not budge. "Let Lodge compromise,"[148] he exclaimed. Even Edith pleaded with him to find a middle ground that would save the treaty. But Wilson simply replied, "Little girl, don't you desert me; that I cannot stand."[149]

On November 19, 1919, the United States Senate voted on ratification of the Treaty of Versailles. In three separate ballots, the treaty failed to win the necessary two-thirds majority. The United States would not join the League of Nations.

"I Must Get Well"

When Edith Wilson told her husband of the defeat, he remarked, "I must get well."[150] But he would never regain the vitality of his youth. His Cabinet met weekly to keep the government running, and Edith made decisions on what matters the president could handle personally without adversely affecting his health. Wilson experienced good days and bad, at times making decisions efficiently and with little effort. He even considered running for a third term as president.

Despite his optimism, those closest to Wilson knew that his political career was over. On March 4, 1921, Republican Warren G. Harding was inaugurated as twenty-ninth President of the United States. Two weeks later the League of Nations came up for one final vote in the Senate. Again it was defeated.

Woodrow and Edith Wilson lived in semi-seclusion in Washington, D.C. until his death on February 3, 1924, at age sixty-seven. Without the United States as a strong member, the League of Nations, Woodrow Wilson's crowning achievement, was an ineffectual organization. Not long after it began operation on January 10, 1920, member nations began forming new military alliances—the kinds of alliances that had already led to a devastating world war, and would help ignite another in less than twenty years.

Woodrow Wilson was a man of many dimensions and contradictions. The most educated president, he was devoutly religious and committed to world peace. Yet he was often stubborn and uncompromising, traits that, in the end, helped keep the United States out of the League of Nations. During his career, Wilson instituted many domestic reforms, but circumstances forced him into a global conflict. Although the League of Nations failed to prevent another world war, Woodrow Wilson never gave up his dream that one day peace would prevail.

☆ Notes ☆

Introduction:
"Lions Led by Donkeys"

1. Richard Holmes, *The Western Front.* New York: TV Books, 1999–2000, p. 140.

Chapter 1: John J. Pershing: General of the Armies

2. Quoted in Donald Smythe, *Pershing: General of the Armies.* Bloomington: Indiana University Press, 1986, p. 238.

3. Quoted in Smythe, *Pershing: General of the Armies*, p. 239.

4. Quoted in Frank E. Vandiver, *Black Jack: The Life and Times of John J. Pershing.* College Station: Texas A&M University Press, 1977, vol. 1, p. 13.

5. Quoted in James G. Harbord, *The American Army in France, 1917–1919.* Boston: Little, Brown, 1936, p. 38.

6. Quoted in Smythe, *Pershing: General of the Armies*, p. 2.

7. Quoted in Vandiver, *Black Jack: The Life and Times of John J. Pershing*, vol. 1, p. 418.

8. John J. Pershing, *My Experiences in the World War.* Blue Ridge Summit, PA: Tab Books, 1989, vol. 1, p. 1.

9. Pershing, *My Experiences in the World War*, vol. 1, p. 1.

10. Quoted in Pershing, *My Experiences in the World War*, vol. 1, p. 38.

11. Quoted in Pershing, *My Experiences in the World War*, vol. 1, p. 38.

12. Quoted in Smythe, *Pershing: General of the Armies*, p. 24.

13. Quoted in Smythe, *Pershing: General of the Armies*, p. 22.

14. Quoted in Gene Smith, *Until the Last Trumpet Sounds.* New York: John Wiley and Sons, 1998, p. 156.

15. Quoted in Smythe, *Pershing: General of the Armies*, p. 101.

16. Quoted in Vandiver, *Black Jack: The Life and Times of John J. Pershing*, vol. 2, p. 949.

17. Quoted in Smythe, *Pershing: General of the Armies*, p. 232.

18. Quoted in Smythe, *Pershing: General of the Armies*, p. 253.

19. Quoted in Smythe, *Pershing: General of the Armies*, p. 272.

20. Quoted in Vandiver, *Black Jack: The Life and Times of John J. Pershing*, vol. 2, p. 1,089.

21. Quoted in Vandiver, *Black Jack: The Life and Times of John J. Pershing*, vol. 2, p. 1,097.

22. Quoted in Smythe, *Pershing: General of the Armies*, p. 309.

Chapter 2: Erich Ludendorff: A Troubled General

23. Quoted in Holger H. Herwig and Neil M. Heyman, *Biographical Dictionary of World War I.* Westport, CT: Greenwood Press, 1982, p. 233.

24. Quoted in Roger Parkinson, *Tormented Warrior: Ludendorff and the Supreme Command.* New York: Stein and Day, 1978, p. 14.

25. Quoted in Parkinson, *Tormented Warrior*, p. 14.

26. Quoted in Parkinson, *Tormented Warrior*, p. 17.

27. Quoted in Correlli Barnett, *The Swordbearers.* New York: William Morrow, 1963, p. 272.

28. Quoted in Barnett, *The Swordbearers*, pp. 271–72.

29. Quoted in Parkinson, *Tormented Warrior*, p. 37.

30. Quoted in Parkinson, *Tormented Warrior*, p. 37.

31. Quoted in Robert B. Asprey, *The German High Command at War.* New York: William Morrow, 1991, p. 86.

32. Quoted in Barnett, *The Swordbearers*, p. 272.

33. Quoted in Parkinson, *Tormented Warrior*, p. 110.

34. Quoted in Asprey, *The German High Command at War*, p. 203.

35. Quoted in Parkinson, *Tormented Warrior*, p. 125.

36. Quoted in Asprey, *The German High Command at War*, p. 309.

37. Quoted in Sir Michael Carver, *The War Lords.* Boston: Little, Brown, 1976, p. 73.

38. Quoted in Barnett, *The Swordbearers*, p. 340.

39. Quoted in Asprey, *The German High Command at War*, p. 448.

40. Quoted in Asprey, *The German High Command at War*, p. 483.

Chapter 3: Philippe Pétain: Hero of Verdun

41. Quoted in Barnett, *The Swordbearers*, p. 217.

42. Quoted in Herbert R. Lottman, *Pétain: Hero or Traitor.* New York: William Morrow, 1985, p. 20.

43. Quoted in Gene Smith, *The Ends of Greatness.* New York: Crown Publishers, 1990, p. 43.

44. Quoted in Lottman, *Pétain: Hero or Traitor*, p. 31.

45. Quoted in Barnett, *The Swordbearers*, p. 198.

46. Quoted in Richard Griffiths, *Pétain: A Biography of Marshal Philippe Pétain of Vichy*, Garden City, NY: Doubleday, 1972, p. xviii.

47. Quoted in Lottman, *Pétain: Hero or Traitor*, p. 38.

48. Quoted in Lottman, *Pétain: Hero or Traitor*, p. 39.

49. Quoted in Griffiths, *Pétain: A Biography of Marshal Philippe Pétain of Vichy*, p. 3.

50. Quoted in Griffiths, *Pétain: A Biography of Marshal Philippe Pétain of Vichy*, p. 4.

51. Quoted in Griffiths, *Pétain: A Biography of Marshal Philippe Pétain of Vichy*, p. 7.

52. Quoted in Smith, *The Ends of Greatness*, p. 49.

53. Quoted in Smith, *The Ends of Greatness*, p. 49.

54. Quoted in Lottman, *Pétain: Hero or Traitor*, p. 50.

55. Quoted in Lottman, *Pétain: Hero or Traitor*, p. 56.

56. Quoted in Carver, *The War Lords*, p. 66.

57. Quoted in Carver, *The War Lords*, p. 70.

58. Quoted in Griffiths, *Pétain: A Biography of Marshal Philippe Pétain of Vichy*, p. 86.

59. Quoted in Griffiths, *Pétain: A Biography of Marshal Philippe Pétain of Vichy*, p. 334.

Chapter 4: William "Billy" Mitchell: Prophet of Airpower

60. Quoted in Isaac Don Levine, *Mitchell: Pioneer of Air Power*. New York: Duell, Sloan and Pearce, 1958, p. 59.

61. Quoted in Levine, *Mitchell: Pioneer of Air Power*, p. 13.

62. Quoted in Burke Davis, *The Billy Mitchell Affair*. New York: Random House, 1967, p. 13.

63. Quoted in Davis, *The Billy Mitchell Affair*, p. 13.

64. Quoted in Davis, *The Billy Mitchell Affair*, p. 13.

65. Quoted in Alfred F. Hurley, *Billy Mitchell: Crusader for Air Power*. New York: Franklin Watts, 1964, p. 3.

66. Ruth Mitchell, *My Brother Bill*. New York: Harcourt, Brace, 1953, p. 28.

67. Quoted in Mitchell, *My Brother Bill*, p. 33.

68. Quoted in Hurley, *Billy Mitchell: Crusader for Air Power*, p. 4.

69. Quoted in Levine, *Mitchell: Pioneer of Air Power*, p. 25.

70. Quoted in Levine, *Mitchell: Pioneer of Air Power*, p. 34.

71. Quoted in Levine, *Mitchell: Pioneer of Air Power*, p. 70.

72. Quoted in Davis, *The Billy Mitchell Affair*, p. 25.

73. Quoted in Davis, *The Billy Mitchell Affair*, p. 26.

74. Quoted in Davis, *The Billy Mitchell Affair*, p. 27.

75. William Mitchell, *Memoirs of World War I*. New York: Random House, 1960, p. 15.

76. Quoted in Davis, *The Billy Mitchell Affair*, p. 30.

77. Mitchell, *Memoirs of World War I*, p. 192.

78. Quoted in Davis, *The Billy Mitchell Affair*, p. 44.

79. Quoted in Levine, *Mitchell: Pioneer of Air Power*, p. 115.

80. Mitchell, *Memoirs of World War I*, p. 210.

81. Mitchell, *Memoirs of World War I*, p. 213.

82. Quoted in Levine, *Mitchell: Pioneer of Air Power*, p. 133.

83. Quoted in Levine, *Mitchell: Pioneer of Air Power*, p. 135.

84. Quoted in Mitchell, *Memoirs of World War I*, p. 250.

85. Quoted in Levine, *Mitchell: Pioneer of Air Power*, p. 165.

86. Quoted in Davis, *The Billy Mitchell Affair*, p. 218.

87. Quoted in Davis, *The Billy Mitchell Affair*, p. 332.

88. Quoted in Levine, *Mitchell: Pioneer of Air Power*, p. 397.

Chapter 5: Douglas Haig: The Gentleman Soldier

89. Quoted in Smith, *The Ends of Greatness*, p. 25.
90. Quoted in Denis Winter, *Haig's Command: A Reassessment*. New York: Viking, 1991, p. 18.
91. Quoted in Gerard J. DeGroot, *Douglas Haig, 1861–1928*. London: Unwin Hyman, p. 16.
92. Quoted in DeGroot, *Douglas Haig, 1861–1928*, p. 19.
93. Quoted in Winter, *Haig's Command: A Reassessment*, p. 19.
94. Quoted in John Terraine, *Ordeal of Victory*. Philadelphia: J. B. Lippincott, 1963, p. 4.
95. Quoted in Terraine, *Ordeal of Victory*, p. 12.
96. Quoted in Terraine, *Ordeal of Victory*, pp. 36–37.
97. Quoted in DeGroot, *Douglas Haig, 1861–1928*, p. 146.
98. Quoted in DeGroot, *Douglas Haig, 1861–1928*, p. 163.
99. Quoted in Terraine, *Ordeal of Victory*, p. 113.
100. Quoted in Terraine, *Ordeal of Victory*, p. 135.
101. Quoted in Terraine, *Ordeal of Victory*, p. 193.
102. Quoted in DeGroot, *Douglas Haig, 1861–1928*, p. 253.
103. Quoted in Terraine, *Ordeal of Victory*, p. 219.
104. Quoted in Smith, *The Ends of Greatness*, p. 77.
105. Quoted in Smith, *The Ends of Greatness*, p. 98.
106. Quoted in Richard Holmes, *The Western Front*, pp. 141–42.
107. Quoted in Terraine, *Ordeal of Victory*, p. 432.
108. Quoted in Terraine, *Ordeal of Victory*, p. 433.
109. Quoted in Carver, *The War Lords*, p. 41.
110. Quoted in Carver, *The War Lords*, p. 42.
111. Winston Churchill, *Great Contemporaries*. Freeport, NY: Books for Libraries Press, 1971, p. 191.

Chapter 6: Ferdinand Foch: The Will to Win

112. Quoted in T. Bentley Mott, trans., *The Memoirs of Marshal Foch*, Garden City, NY: Doubleday, Doran, 1931, pp. xxxiii, xxxiv.
113. Quoted in Mott, *The Memoirs of Marshal Foch*, pp. xxxiii, xxxv.
114. Quoted in Mott, *The Memoirs of Marshal Foch*, p. xxxvi.
115. Quoted in James Marshall-Cornwall, *Foch as Military Commander*. New York: Crane, Russak, 1972, p. 6.
116. Quoted in Marshall-Cornwall, *Foch as Military Commander*, p. 15.
117. Quoted in Marshall-Cornwall, *Foch as Military Commander*, p. 16.
118. Charles H. L. Johnston, *Famous Generals of the Great War*. Freeport, New York: Books for Libraries Press, 1970, p. 100.
119. Quoted in Mott, *The Memoirs of Marshal Foch*, p. 47.
120. Quoted in Carver, *The War Lords*, p. 128.

121. Quoted in Marshall-Cornwall, *Foch as Military Commander*, p. 99.

122. Quoted in Mott, *The Memoirs of Marshal Foch*, p. 15.

123. Quoted in Marshall-Cornwall, *Foch as Military Commander*, pp. 146–47.

124. Quoted in Mott, *The Memoirs of Marshal Foch*, p. 236.

125. Quoted in Mott, *The Memoirs of Marshal Foch*, p. 236.

126. Quoted in Mott, *The Memoirs of Marshal Foch*, p. 368.

127. Quoted in Asprey, *The German High Command at War*, p. 448.

128. Quoted in Mott, *The Memoirs of Marshal Foch*, p. 463.

129. Quoted in Stanley Weintraub, *A Stillness Heard Round the World*. New York: Oxford University Press, 1985, p. 53.

130. Quoted in Weintraub, *A Stillness Heard Round The World*, p. 159.

Chapter 7: Woodrow Wilson: Crusader for Peace

131. Quoted in Jan Willem Schulte Nordholt, *Woodrow Wilson: A Life for World Peace*. Berkeley: University of California Press, 1991, p. 391.

132. Quoted in Thomas J. Knock, *To End All Wars*. New York: Oxford University Press, 1992, p. 3.

133. Quoted in Edwin A. Weinstein, *Woodrow Wilson: A Medical and Psychological Biography*. Princeton, NJ: Princeton University Press, 1981, p. 31.

134. Quoted in Nordholt, *Woodrow Wilson: A Life for World Peace*, p. 13.

135. Quoted in Nordholt, *Woodrow Wilson: A Life for World Peace*, p. 14.

136. Quoted in Nordholt, *Woodrow Wilson: A Life for World Peace*, p. 83.

137. Quoted in Knock, *To End All Wars*, p. 11.

138. Quoted in Nordholt, *Woodrow Wilson: A Life for World Peace*, p. 101.

139. Quoted in Nordholt, *Woodrow Wilson: A Life for World Peace*, p. 121.

140. Quoted in Nordholt, *Woodrow Wilson: A Life for World Peace*, p. 133.

141. Quoted in Gene Smith, *When the Cheering Stopped: The Last Years of Woodrow Wilson*. New York: William Morrow, 1964, p. 9.

142. Quoted in Nordholt, *Woodrow Wilson: A Life for World Peace*, p. 137.

143. Quoted in Weinstein, *Woodrow Wilson: A Medical and Psychological Biography*, p. 284.

144. Quoted in Smith, *When the Cheering Stopped*, p. 43.

145. Quoted in Weinstein, *Woodrow Wilson: A Medical and Psychological Biography*, p. 335.

146. Quoted in Smith, *When the Cheering Stopped*, p. 80.

147. Quoted in Weinstein, *Woodrow Wilson: A Medical and Psychological Biography*, p. 356.

148. Quoted in Nordholt, *Woodrow Wilson: A Life for World Peace*, p. 401.

149. Quoted in Nordholt, *Woodrow Wilson: A Life for World Peace*, p. 402.

150. Quoted in Smith, *When the Cheering Stopped*, p. 120.

★ For Further Reading ★

Ezra Bowen, *Knights of the Air*. Alexandria, VA: Time-Life Books, 1980. An abundantly illustrated history of the evolution of the airplane as a weapon in World War I. Part of Time-Life's *Epic of Flight* series.

Trevor Nevitt Dupuis, *The Military Lives of Hindenburg and Ludendorff of Imperial Germany*. New York: Franklin Watts, 1970. The story of the two generals who ran Germany's military machine in the second half of World War I, and the political influence they wielded.

——, *Summation: Strategic and Combat Leadership*. New York: Franklin Watts, 1967. This compendium includes evaluations of World War I's principal military leaders, a chronology of the war, and statistics on the ultimate cost, both monetary and human, of the war.

Alistair Horne, *The Price of Glory: Verdun 1916*. New York: St. Martin's Press, 1963. One of the best histories of the Battle of Verdun, with more than 250 personal accounts by participants on both sides of the battle.

Alfred F. Hurley, *Billy Mitchell: Crusader for Air Power*. New York: Franklin Watts, 1964. A critical yet readable study of the life and career of Billy Mitchell, written by a U.S. Air Force officer.

David Jacobs, *An American Conscience: Woodrow Wilson's Search for World Peace*. New York: Harper and Row, 1973. The complete life story of Woodrow Wilson and his quest for peace.

James T. Rogers, *Woodrow Wilson: Visionary for Peace*. New York: Facts On File, 1997. This book examines Woodrow Wilson's creation of the League of Nations.

Stewart Ross, *Causes and Conseqences of World War I*. Austin, TX: Raintree Steck-Vaughn, 1998. This book examines the political forces leading up to World War I and the results of the devastating conflict.

Donald Summerville, *World War I*. Austin, TX: Raintree Steck-Vaughn, 1998. A general overview of the war from the publisher's *History of Warfare* series. Includes a short glossary and bibliography.

Frank E. Vandiver, *Illustrious Americans: John J. Pershing*. Morristown, NJ: Silver Burdett, 1967. An illustrated biography that includes photographs, artwork, and excerpts from Pershing's unpublished memoirs.

Harold Cecil Vaughn, *The Versailles Treaty*. New York: Franklin Watts, 1975. The story of the Paris Peace Conference and the negotiations that ultimately produced a treaty that ended the war—and paved the way for another.

☆ Works Consulted ☆

Robert B. Asprey, *The German High Command at War*. New York: William Morrow, 1991. An in-depth history of Paul von Hindenburg and Erich Ludendorff, the two men who led Germany through World War I and how they ultimately presided over Germany's downfall.

Correlli Barnett, *The Swordbearers*. New York: William Morrow, 1963. Profiles of Philippe Pétain, Erich Ludendorff, and two other World War I leaders and how their characters affected the war and its outcome.

Sir Michael Carver, ed., *The War Lords*. Boston: Little, Brown, 1976. Short biographies of forty-three of the highest level military commanders of World War I and World War II.

Winston S. Churchill, *Great Contemporaries*. 1937. Reprint. Freeport, NY: Books for Libraries Press, 1971. Biographies of British statesmen and military commanders, written by Churchill from 1929 to 1937.

Burke Davis, *The Billy Mitchell Affair*. New York: Random House, 1967. A well-written biography that concentrates on Mitchell's postwar activities, especially his court-martial and his investigations on Japanese airpower.

Gerard DeGroot, *Douglas Haig, 1861–1928*. London: Unwin Hyman, 1988. A thorough recounting of the life of Britain's much maligned World War I general.

Richard Griffiths, *Pétain: A Biography of Marshal Philippe Pétain of Vichy*. Garden City, NY: Doubleday, 1972. The first complete biography of Pétain in English, examining the controversial general and his reasons for his collaboration with the Nazis in World War II.

James G. Harbord, *The American Army in France, 1917–1919*. Boston: Little, Brown, 1936. An eyewitness account of the American Expeditionary Forces in France, written by General Pershing's chief of staff.

Holger H. Herwig and Neil M. Heyman, *Biographical Dictionary of World War I*. Westport, CT: Greenwood Press, 1982. Short biographical sketches of virtually every major personality of World War I. Also includes a brief overview of the war and an extensive bibliography.

Richard Holmes, *The Western Front*. New York: TV Books, 2000. A vivid account of how the ordinary soldier fought and died on the Western Front. Filled with fascinating details and first person accounts.

Charles Johnston, *Famous Generals of the Great War*. 1919. Reprint. Freeport, NY: Books for Libraries Press, 1970. Written shortly after the war ended, Johnston profiles the most prominent generals of the conflict.

Thomas Knock, *To End All Wars.* New York: Oxford University Press, 1992. An in-depth account of Woodrow Wilson's diplomacy, from his earliest writings to his quest for world peace during and after World War I.

Isaac Don Levine, *Mitchell: Pioneer of Air Power.* Rev. ed. New York: Duell, Sloan and Pearce, 1958. A detailed, definitive biography of General Billy Mitchell.

Herbert R. Lottman, *Pétain: Hero or Traitor: The Untold Story.* New York: William Morrow, 1985. Based on secret documents and eyewitness accounts, this biography concentrates on Pétain's life after World War I and his Vichy years.

Sir James Handyside Marshall-Cornwall, *Foch as Military Commander.* New York: Crane, Russak, 1972. General Marshall-Cornwall uses official documents, memoirs, diaries, and personal papers to recount Foch's life and military career.

Ruth Mitchell, *My Brother Bill.* New York: Harcourt, Brace, 1953. Personal reminiscences about Billy Mitchell written by his sister.

William Mitchell, *Memoirs of World War I.* New York: Random House, 1960. Billy Mitchell's firsthand account of his wartime activities, based on the diaries he kept during the war. Originally appeared in serial form in *Liberty Magazine.*

T. Bentley Mott, trans., *Memoirs of Marshal Foch.* Garden City, NY: Doubleday, Doran, 1931. Mott, serving as liaison officer between Foch and General Pershing, worked at Foch's headquarters during the war and offers a personal account of Foch's life.

Jan Willem Schulte Nordholt, *Woodrow Wilson: A Life for World Peace.* Translated by Herbert H. Rowen. Berkeley: University of California Press, 1991. An internationally known Dutch historian examines Woodrow Wilson's life and the moral and religious bases for his desire for world peace.

Roger Parkinson, *Tormented Warrior: Ludendorff and the Supreme Command.* New York: Stein and Day, 1978. The author tries to salvage his subject's reputation by uncovering what he believes are the real reasons behind Ludendorff's eccentric personality.

John J. Pershing, *My Experiences in the World War.* 2 vols. 1931. Reprint. Blue Ridge Summit, PA: Tab Books, 1989. Pulitzer Prize–winning memoir of "Black Jack" Pershing's experiences during the war.

Frank C. Platt, comp., *Great Battles of World War I in the Air.* New York: Weathervane Books, 1966. This book features first-hand accounts of World War I air battles, and includes excerpts from Billy Mitchell's war diary.

Gene Smith, *The Ends of Greatness.* New York: Crown Publishers, 1990. Biographies of four great men—including Douglas Haig and Philippe Pétain—living at the end of the nineteenth century and coping with the coming of the twentieth.

————, *Until the Last Trumpet Sounds.* New York: John Wiley and Sons, 1998. An interesting and readable account of General Pershing's life, including information about the military careers of his son and his grandson, who was killed in Vietnam and now rests beside the general at Arlington National Cemetery.

————, *When the Cheering Stopped: The Last Years of Woodrow Wilson.* New York: William Morrow, 1964. The story of Woodrow Wilson's final years, including his quest for a lasting peace and the role his second wife played after Wilson's debilitating stroke.

Donald Smythe, *Pershing: General of the Armies.* Bloomington: Indiana University Press, 1986. The second of two Pershing biographies by Smythe, this book focuses on the general's war years to his death in 1948. Smythe's first volume, *Guerrilla Warrior*, recounts Pershing's early life.

John Terraine, *Ordeal of Victory.* Philadelphia: J. B. Lippincott, 1963. A military biography of General Douglas Haig that analyzes his strengths as well as his weaknesses as a commander.

John Toland, *No Man's Land.* Garden City, NY: Doubleday, 1980. Toland, a Pulitzer Prize–winning author, tells the story of 1918, the final year of World War I and the events that led up to the armistice.

Frank E. Vandiver, *Black Jack: The Life and Times of John J. Pershing.* 2 vols. College Station: Texas A&M University Press, 1977. A definitive biography of John J. Pershing, the soldier and the man.

Edwin A. Weinstein, *Woodrow Wilson: A Medical and Psychological Biography.* Princeton, NJ: Princeton University Press, 1981. The author, a medical doctor, describes Wilson's physical and psychological makeup, and examines the role that illness played in the shaping of Wilson's administration.

Stanley Weintraub, *A Stillness Heard Round the World.* New York: Oxford University Press, 1985. A dramatic recounting of the end of World War I and the armistice.

Denis Winter, *Haig's Command: A Reassessment.* New York: Viking, 1991. The author reexamines the official myths surrounding Haig's career by using previously unavailable sources.

⋆ **Picture Credits** ⋆

Cover photos: © Bettmann/Corbis (center), Library of Congress (top right), © Underwood and Underwood/Corbis (lower left)

Archive Photos, 16, 39, 46, 51, 53, 61, 67, 71, 79 85, 86, 94

© Bettmann/Corbis, 5, 19, 27, 37, 48, 49, 50, 55, 59, 76, 83, 91, 92

© Corbis, 8, 11, 14, 20, 35, 64, 87

Leonard de Selva/Corbis, 28

Express Newspapers/Archive Photos, 45

© Eye Ubiquitous/Corbis, 63

© Hulton-Deutsch Collection/Corbis, 7, 9, 24, 25, 31, 36, 40, 43, 62, 69, 73, 74, 80, 81

Library of Congress, 30

© The Mariner's Museum/Corbis, 57

National Archives, 12

The Pennsylvania Academy of the Fine Arts, Bequest of Mrs. Joseph Harrison, Jr., 22

© Lee Snider; Lee Snider/Corbis, 89

© Joseph Sohm: ChromoSome Inc./Corbis, 13

☆ About the Author ☆

Craig E. Blohm has been writing magazine articles on historical subjects for children for more than fifteen years. He has also written for social studies textbooks and conducted workshops in writing history for children. A native of Chicago, he has worked for more than twenty-five years in the field of television production, serving in various positions including production manager, writer, producer, and director. He is currently the Television and Radio Production Coordinator at Purdue University Calumet in Hammond, Indiana. He and his wife Desiree live in Tinley Park, Illinois, and have two sons, Eric and Jason.